10/20/06

Michael Stone
    Best Wishes to you + your
family. Thank you for the help and
friendship you have been to me.

Stanley Backman

In His Own Words

The Story of Stanley Parkman

by

Stanley Parkman

Bloomington, IN  Milton Keynes, UK

authorHOUSE®

AuthorHouse™
1663 Liberty Drive, Suite 200
Bloomington, IN 47403
www.authorhouse.com
Phone: 1-800-839-8640

AuthorHouse™ UK Ltd.
500 Avebury Boulevard
Central Milton Keynes, MK9 2BE
www.authorhouse.co.uk
Phone: 08001974150

This book is a work of non-fiction. Unless otherwise noted, the author
and the publisher make no explicit guarantees as to the accuracy of
the information contained in this book and in some cases, names of
people and places have been altered to protect their privacy.

First published by AuthorHouse 8/1/2006

ISBN: 1-4259-4698-4 (sc)

Library of Congress Control Number: 2006905674

Printed in the United States of America
Bloomington, Indiana

This book is printed on acid-free paper.

But I'll report it
Where Senators shall mingle tears with smiles;
Where great patricians shall attend and shrug,
I' th' end admire; where ladies shall be frighted,
And, gladly quaked, hear more; where the dull
       tribunes,
That with the fusty plebeians hate thine honors;
Shall say against their hearts, "We thank the gods
Our Rome hath such a soldier."

--Shakespeare, *Coriolanus*

The Lord is my Shepherd, I shall not want...

Contents

CHAPTER I

FATHER AND MOTHER

My mother died when I was five years old. My dad and I were never that close or talkative about the five years between her death and his marriage to my stepmother. I do know that my mother died of tuberculosis in 1920.

David Stanley Parkman, Jr. was born on July 17, 1915, to David Stanley Parkman and Alice Crawford Parkman. Woodrow Wilson was president; World War I was a year old; the Boston Red Sox won the World Series, and the boll weevil was in Georgia. His birth came at a poor economic time in the lives of most Americans living in the south, and his family was no exception.

His father met Alice Crawford of Columbus while he was living in the small town of Cusseta, Georgia, and clerking in a country store. They began a courtship and were married a short time later. An account of their nuptials appeared in a Columbus newspaper:

> A wedding of interest to many friends on Wednesday evening was that of Miss Alice Golden Crawford and Mr. David Stanley Parkman, of Glen Alter, Ga., which was quietly solemnized

1

at the home of the bride's mother, Mrs. Nina Crawford, 402 Broad Street, in the presence of only the relatives and most intimate friends of the contracting parties.

In the parlor where the ceremony was performed there was an altar of palms and ferns, and the decorations of smilax and white oleander were most effective.

First to enter was the matron of honor, Mrs. Roy Crawford, who wore a dainty white lingerie gown and carried pink carnations.

Miss Phoebe Crawford was her sister's maid of honor, and she wore a lovely costume of lingerie and lace. Her flowers were also pink carnations.

The bride entered with her brother, Mr. Roy Crawford, by whom she was given in marriage. She was lovely in a traveling suit of midnight blue moiré and burnt leghorn hat with trimmings of blue velvet. She carried a bouquet of Easter lilies showered with lilies of the valley.

Mr. Parkman, attended by Mr. Paul Heard as best man, met his bride at the altar, and Rev. Wragg performed the ceremony, using the ring service.

During the evening Mr. and Mrs. Parkman left for the groom's home in Glen Alter.

The bride is a young woman of unusual charm, and she has many friends who regret that she will make her home away from Columbus.

> Mr. Parkman is a prosperous young business
> man of Glen Alter, and has many friends who
> congratulate him most heartily. He is a cousin of
> Mr. and Mrs. J. A. Beard of this city.

The couple moved to Glen Alter, Georgia, where Parkman had secured a job as manager of a 5000-acre plantation run by the Bergen Lumber Company of Columbus, Georgia. This was to be a new and better life for them despite the dismal economic conditions of the county itself. At the time, unemployment had reached a high 8.5%.

Running the plantation was all-consuming work. The soil was poor, and plowing it was tough. Timber was cut with crosscut saws, and logs were dragged to the mill by teams of mules. Consequently, Parkman spent most of his day in the saddle, riding back and forth from the sawmill to the cotton and corn fields. And in the evening, after working hours, he opened the commissary supplying necessities for himself and the field hands for an hour or two before returning home to Alice.

All of the workers were black men who lived on the plantation with their families, as did the Parkmans. The year was 1915, and on July 17 Alice gave birth to a son, named David Stanley after his father. Three years later another son was born, Nathaniel Toliver, whom they called Tol. Tol's birth, in fact, became his older brother's first memory. The family had traveled to Alice's parents' home in Columbus for the blessed event. Over eighty years later, Stanley recalled that he was playing in the yard when someone came onto the porch of the house and announced he had a brother

But the young family's joy was to be short-lived. Within two years of Tol's birth, Alice was diagnosed with Tuberculosis. She sought a cure at the only sanitarium in the region, in distant Alto. After a period of seclusion and rest, Alice's condition worsened, and she died.

"That's my next real memory after my brother was born," Stanley said. "I remember when my aunt and a few other relatives packed up for her to go to the hospital. After that, I never saw her again."

The family's grief became two-fold the day of Alice's funeral. The brothers were sent to stay with their father's sister, Maxie Gordy, for the day, and while playing with cousins in the yard, Tol ran into a back gate's hook latch, putting out his right eye. Their father returned to Glen Alter a widower with two small sons, one in pain and in need of nursing. In addition to the plantation, he now had sole responsibility for them. The wife of a black field hand took on the role of their cooking and cleaning and kept an eye on the boys during the day. Her children became the boys' playmates, and soon they fell into the new routine. But the stress was often more than Parkman could bear.

Stanley recalled the time, saying, "I can remember nights hearing him in his room, which adjoined ours, praying and asking God to help him rear us two boys right, and do everything else he had to do. Talking about it chokes me up to this day."

Although plantation life did not include a church, Parkman relied on two books for spiritual encouragement: the Bible and *The Pilgrim's Progress.* In time, however, organized religion would become a part of all their lives.

CHAPTER II

BOYHOOD

My father had no telephone, no running water,
no motorized vehicle to travel in, nobody to keep
house and do the cooking. It's hard to imagine a
young man able to hold up in those circumstances.
After he died, I repeatedly told myself and other
folks that he was the best man I'd ever known.

Stanley was late starting school, and when he did he was
among a dozen other white children from the surrounding
community ranging from first through seventh grade who were
taught in a one-room building by one teacher.

He attended school through the week, helped his father
when he could, and on Sunday he reveled in the pleasures of
boyhood. Though toys were scarce, Stanley and Tol enjoyed
a pet goat that slept under their six-foot high front porch. But
Stanley wanted a cart for his hoofed friend and was inventive
enough to ask his father to have his sawmill workers cut four
wheels off of a pine log so that he could build his own.

"I know I hounded him to death about it," Stanley recalled.
"But he never did get around to getting me those wheels, so I
never got to build my cart."

Whereas Sunday was a day of boyhood fun for Stanley,
it was mostly a day of rest for his father who usually took

a long afternoon nap. One Sunday, while his father slept, Stanley wandered down to the nearby railroad shed. There he found a group of field hands shooting craps and using language he'd never heard. Fascinated, he stayed to watch and listen. In the meantime, Parkman awoke and discovered Stanley missing.

"He found me down there watching this group shooting craps and cussing," Stanley said. "By that time, somehow or other, he had a buggy whip in his hand. I remember very distinctly that he whipped me with that buggy whip all the way from the railroad shed to the house. It must've been a hundred yards, and I was jumping every step. But before this, he told that bunch of blacks to get out of that place and go home and never let him catch them there again. I never learned to shoot craps, never learned to play poker, never learned any kind of gambling from that time to this, so help me."

But as strict as he could be, Parkman had a soft side. He managed to make Christmastime memorable for his sons. There was one in particular, Stanley recalled: "My father gave me a pony—saddle, bridle, all of that. I don't know where he got it or how much it cost him. You can imagine what a great Christmas that was."

The following summer his father accidentally drove a nail through a board into his kneecap. Bleeding, he ordered a field hand to ride Stanley's pony to the nearest telephone at the Christopher community five miles away and call the doctor. After what seemed like a long time, the man returned on foot with good and bad news.

The good news was that the doctor was coming fast as he could in horse and buggy. The bad news was that Stanley's pony was dead. "The fellow had ridden it so hard that halfway back it fell over," Stanley said with a chuckle. "He rode my pony to death!"

Years later Stanley returned to Glen Alter, and later he recalled:

I remember three buildings from Glen Alter. The house we lived in, the commissary, and the one-room schoolhouse on the other side of the railroad from the house and commissary. Back a couple of years ago my sister who lives at Cuthbert, at my request, found out if we could go and visit Glen Alter—I had never been back there since my dad remarried and went to Hardaway. And that was eighty years ago. But I remembered the location of the buildings.

My grandson Mark was keenly interested in this, and on one of his trips home, we went down there. My sister had found out that the 5000 acres is now a hunting preserve owned by I-forget- the-name-of-the-company that grows pine trees on it. It's under a fence and gate, and lock and key. And there's a man there who makes sure there are no fires and that sort of thing. But we made arrangements with him to meet us there and let us in the gate and show us around.

Would you believe that the only three buildings that are left standing are those three buildings! The old house is badly dilapidated, but it was just as I remembered it. It had a big front porch six feet off the ground and slanted to the backside. There was a sitting room and two bedrooms—my dad's room and the room that we boys were in, a little eating area, and then a catwalk between that part of the house and the kitchen. They built them like that for fire protection. There was a back porch, and the well was at one end it. Now, still standing enough to be recognized was the kitchen, the walk, and the rest of the rooms!

The commissary is now a hunting lodge and is almost like it was, in pretty good shape for people who come down there. And he took us up through the woods. You have to go through a lot of brush and briars and trees, but we got to the old school-house. And the only change to it was over the years they had put a partition right through the middle, making it a two-room schoolhouse instead of one. We took pictures and we brought bricks back from the old house. Many of the kids have those.

CHAPTER III

A NEW MOTHER

When my father started going with my stepmother, she lived at Christopher. Her parents, Mr. and Mrs. Charlton Johnson, had a little country store there. As to how they met, I just don't know. Times were hard then and getting worse all the time.

Frances Johnson was the only child of Mr. and Mrs. Charlton Johnson and had graduated from Shorter College with a degree in education. When she began dating Parkman, who was fifteen years her senior, she was in her second year of teaching school. Her parents were against their marrying, but she and Parkman had other ideas.

The wedding was held at a small Baptist church in Cusseta. Stanley noted the contrast of his tall, muscular father beside his petite stepmother as they made their vows.

Stanley recalled that "when the ceremony was over and they started down the aisle, she somehow wasn't walking fast enough to suit him, so he just picked her up in his arms and walked right out that door." He sat her in the Ford Model-T he'd just bought and drove away as the guests waved and Stanley and Tol watched.

The newlyweds went to Hardaway in North Florida, where they intended to start their life together. Parkman left his sons with their Aunt Maxie in Cusseta until he and his bride could get settled.

The mother of Parkman and his sister Maxie had also died young. Like Stanley, Parkman had been only five at the time of her passing. Their father had lost a leg fighting in the Civil War, and Maxie, the oldest of three children, had to care for two younger brothers. She was a schoolteacher, her husband a rural mail carrier. Stanley recalled that every morning his aunt would leave for school in one horse and buggy, her husband for his mail route in another.

"They were a two horse-and-buggy family," he joked.

After two months, Parkman returned to take his sons to their new home in Florida. "We went down there in the Model-T," Stanley remembered. "It was about 225 miles, and we did it all in one day on mostly dirt roads. My dad liked to leave before daylight. He had a saying, 'I like to be driving into daylight, not into dark.'"

Thus began the Hardaway years.

CHAPTER IV

SETTLING IN AT HARDAWAY

> Hardaway was a big plantation-type operation.
> Its primary purpose was to furnish housing for
> construction workers. But there was also extensive
> farming. They grew tobacco in the summertime
> and cabbage in the winter and spring on the same
> acreage.

Stanley Parkman, Jr., was ten years old in 1925, the year his
father married Frances Johnson. His mother had been dead
for five years, and now he and his younger brother were in an
unfamiliar place.

The community of Hardaway was owned by the Hardaway
Construction Company out of Columbus, which had contracts
for building bridges across the Flint River in Bainbridge and
dams at nearby Lake Talquin, a large, man-made body of water
between Tallahassee and Quincy, Florida.

Parkman's new position managing the commissary serving
the Hardaway community was similar to the one he'd held at
Glen Alter. Although much of the South was not faring well, the
economy of Hardaway was thriving because it was at the center
hub of major construction and farming projects.

A tall windmill supplemented by a gasoline engine pumped water and also generated electricity for most of the houses at Hardaway. Even though electricity was restricted to the evening hours, the Parkman family's living conditions were much improved from those at Glen Alter. Stanley recalled, "There I was, ten years old and this is the first time I had seen electricity in a home. And we had running water, too, a telephone, and even an indoor toilet!"

The boys found it easy to settle into their new environment. They became friends with the other children of the community and with those of Mr. and Mrs. Hardaway, the owners of the construction

company. They lived nearby in the largest and finest house Stanley had ever seen.

"When the Hardaways went back to Columbus during the summer, they'd often leave their two children behind, and my step-mother and Tol and I would move in with them for a week or so. We'd play in that big house, and at night my step-mother would read books to all of us kids. Oh, did we enjoy that." He also enjoyed playing tennis on the Hardaway's clay courts.

Frances enjoyed reading and encouraged her family to do the same. Her formal education was an asset not only for Stanley and Tol, but also for Parkman, whose schooling had reached only the sixth grade. "My dad's education was limited," Stanley reflected. "But he was smart and very capable, as evidenced by the responsible jobs he had."

The schoolhouse at Hardaway was within walking distance. One of Stanley's first assignments was to memorize a Bible verse. Not knowing which one to choose, he asked his step-mother for advice. Stanley recalled that without blinking an eye she said, "'I know the perfect verse for you. *'The Lord is my shepherd, I shall not want.'* I memorized it, and the next day I recited it as proudly as anybody."

Years later, this verse would be the first line Stanley typed on every Linotype machine he owned.

CHAPTER V

HARDAWAY DAYS

My stepmother was a pretty strict disciplinarian. My dad had been, too, at Glen Alter, and I was afraid of him. But by this time he had softened a bit. I've come to believe he had been a pretty tough customer because he was responsible for raising two little boys without a wife to help him.

Within a couple of years of moving to Hardaway, Frances gave birth to their first child, a daughter. Mrs. Hardaway had grown very fond of the Parkmans, and as soon as she saw the new baby in its mother's arms, she urged them to call her Frances, too. A second daughter, Jane, followed a few years later. The Parkman family had doubled in size.

Stanley was now twelve and responsible for his share of the work. "My step-mother loved growing flowers in the yard," he said, "and since there weren't any gas tillers then, the only way she could get her flower beds prepared for planting was with a shovel and a hoe. So I was her tiller."

It was also when he was twelve that he had his first serious illness, a leg ailment that kept him bedridden for weeks. Exacerbating his recovery was a sudden case of appendicitis that

13

landed him in the hospital in nearby Quincy. He spent another few weeks recuperating there after an appendectomy.

"They said I almost died," he recalled. "I have the darndest scar you've ever seen from that appendix operation. When doctors see that place they ask, 'What in the world did they operate on you with, a pick and shovel?'"

Stanley's recovery put him behind in his school work, but he doubled his efforts and eventually caught up. When he was again feeling able, he was given the post of herding cattle from pasture to to pasture on horseback. He took so much pleasure in doing this that he dreamed of being a full-time cowboy for Mr. Hardaway the rest of his life.

One of those afternoons the sky grew dark and ominous, and Stanley hurried to corral the cattle near a gate that led to the barn. But as he was about to open it, a great bolt of lightning struck the fence, electrocuting the animals. Stanley recounted, "When I was finally able to regain my senses, I realized that fourteen of my cows were dead on the ground. *Fourteen!"*

That fall, the small school at Hardaway was consolidated with the larger one three miles away at Mt. Pleasant. Rather than having the children walk six miles roundtrip each day, a local man built a bus body out of wood and mounted it on a Ford truck frame.

Soon Stanley was one of the fifth grade at Mt. Pleasant under the wise wing of Miss Parker, who was the sister of newly elected Governor Parker. He did well through the eighth grade, and when he started high school he volunteered for the newly organized football team, much to the chagrin of his father who thought such play was a waste of good working hours.

"They didn't provide transportation," Stanley recalled, "so those of us from Hardaway had to walk home after the grueling practices. Dad didn't like it because it cut into my time milking cows and gathering stove wood, and I'd worry about that all the way home."

The coach was a young man who had recently played at the University of Alabama. He tried his best to teach his teenage team the basics of the game and to get them into winning shape. But he had a tough time of it. During one practice he became so exasperated by their lack of progress that he lined them up at one end of the practice field and challenged any and all of them to tackle him. Stanley recalled that the coach backed off about twenty yards, tucked the football under his arm, and ran right at them. "Everybody scrambled to get of the way," he said, "but me. "Like a fool I stood my ground, and he hit me head on and ran right over me! Knocked me out!" When Stanley came to, the coach helped him to his feet and congratulated him.

As the years passed, Stanley grew tall and slender like his father, and his dream of being a cowboy faded as he was given new responsibilities. One of these was working in the shade tobacco fields.

The soil and climate of Hardaway were ideal for this tobacco. It was grown in only two other places, Cuba and Turkey, but more was produced in and about Hardaway. The tobacco was called "shade" because it had to be grown beneath three layers of cheesecloth to protect the leaves from direct sunlight and insects. Shade tobacco was used exclusively for the outside wrappers of fine cigars and blemishes of any kind were unacceptable.

Stanley described the growing process: "You'd set out those plants in rows three or four feet apart beneath the cheesecloth shade supported by wires running seven feet above. When the plants were about twelve inches high, you'd have to loop a string around the stalk at the bottom, and then hand it up to somebody standing on a bench who tied it around that overhead wire."

The process would continue until several acres were planted. Stanley worked alongside regular field hands beneath the thick layers of cheesecloth from early morning through the hot, Florida day and on until dusk for $3.50 a week.

"And that wasn't paid in cash money," he said. "You got it on a ticket, and the store would punch out how much you bought, so you had to spend it at the commissary my dad was running."

When the tobacco ripened, the leaves were carefully broken off the stalks and taken to a barn where women workers used needles and string to bunch many together. The bunches were handed up to men standing on slats in the top of the barn who hung them on wires as close together as possible. After a level was full, they moved to the next level and did the same until the barn was filled from top to bottom. Then the leaves were left to cure.

"I hung a lot of those bunches during harvest season because I was tall and young and agile," said Stanley. "But it was sure tough work."

CHAPTER VI

INTRODUCTION TO FAITH

The Baptist church at Hardaway was not very active when we moved there, so my dad and step-mother did what they could to increase attendance and improve the building. One of the first summers I had plenty of time and nothing else to do, so I helped repaint the church.

The Hardaway Baptist church was a one-room structure that stood beside the school, not far from the Parkman house. Led by Frances, the family took on the responsibility of building the congregation and improving the condition of the building. To create space for separate Sunday school classes they hung curtains made of bed sheets that could be opened up for the worship service. They arranged for Reverend Wattenberger, the pastor of Chattahoochee Baptist Church, to preach for their small congregation every other Sunday afternoon. Mrs. McDonald, who was a staff member at the Florida Baptist Convention in Jacksonville, came and conducted study courses and training sessions.

The Parkmans welcomed Mrs. McDonald as a house guest during her visits. For several summers she assisted in the development of the church, and during one of them escorted a group of young people to Panama City Beach for a weekend. It was the first time Stanley saw the Gulf. "While we were there we had a discussion group," he recalled. "Mrs. McDonald asked some of us questions. She smiled at me and said, 'Stanley, you're about six feet, aren't you?' But I thought she said sixteen, and I answered, 'Yes, ma'am, I will be next week!' Everybody got a big kick out of the fact that I was growing in a hurry!"

It was at Hardaway that he made his profession of faith and joined the church. Reverend Wattenberger baptized him at the Glen Julia Pool and Springs in Mt. Pleasant. "It was the coldest water in the world," Stanley remembered.

This marked the beginning of his life-long faith in God and his service in the Baptist church.

CHAPTER VII

MOVE TO RIVER JUNCTION

This was 1931, and the Depression was bad everywhere. The Hardaway Corporation finished those major projects of bridges and dams and shut down everything, including my dad's job running the commissary. So we moved to River Junction.

River Junction was the south section of Chattahoochee, Florida, where railroads converged. Railroad jobs, therefore, were plentiful and provided the major payroll for the area. The community consisted of only a few merchants, a post office, and the railroad yard.

The Parkman's wanted to start a business and found the least expensive building they could. They planned to run a typical country store, but Parkman had the idea of including what he called "the chicken-and-egg business".

Since very little money was in circulation, he decided to barter with farmers in the area. Using a pick-up truck, he delivered feed in exchange for eggs and culled chickens. It wasn't long before word got around, and he developed popular routes through parts of Gadsden and adjoining Jackson County.

The business was successful, but time-consuming and te-dious. Every egg had to be candled, a process in which it was held up to a light to establish its quality. The chickens had to be killed and dressed using a method that was messy and unsanitary by today's standards.

"You didn't cut their heads off," Stanley recalled. "You didn't ring their necks like we normally would. You hung that chicken up by its feet on wires out in the back yard, and you took a sharp pointed knife and held its mouth open with one hand and punctured the roof of its mouth up into its brain and killed it immdiately. The blood came out of that incision you made."

After the chickens were killed, they were plunged into a pot of boiling water, their feathers plucked, and their entrails were removed.

A mile north of River Junction at Chattahoochee was Florida's only mental hospital. Whereas the railroad yard was the major employer for River Junction, the hospital was for Chattahoochee. Parkman negotiated a contract with the institution to provide fresh chicken and eggs. "He'd refrigerate the meat," Stanley recalled, "and deliver it to the hospital. They paid him actual money. It was a great deal in those days for my dad."

But everyone was not so fortunate. The worsening depression forced Frances' parents, Mr. and Mrs. Johnson, to move in with the Parkman's following the failure of their store in Christopher. They brought with them Elizabeth Chason, a young lady whom they had unofficially adopted years before while Frances was away at college.

Elizabeth was older than Stanley by only a couple of years, and together they enrolled at Chattahoochee High School. The family attended Chattahoochee Baptist Church, which, along with the high school, was located between River Junction and Chattahoochee and within walking distance of both.

Life continued reasonably well for the newly-extended family. Frances and her father supervised the store while Parkman ran his routes. Mrs. Johnson managed the household chores, and everyone had a place. But the house was too small to accommodate nine people, and Stanley was growing restless.

CHAPTER VIII

CHATTAHOOCHEE HIGH

We had a high school basketball team that was pretty good because we had six or eight boys as tall as I was. We played on an outdoor clay court, but there was no money in the school budget for a basketball. So Mr. Williams bought it himself, and even coached us most of the time. That was something I'll never forget.

Mr. J.E. Williams was the principal of Chattahoochee High School. He had been educated at Peabody College in Nashville, Tennessee, and was intelligent and kind even though his hair was unusual.

"He wore his hair like a ghost," Stanley said. "It was a big pile of grey and never looked combed, except it was."

Principal William's specialty was American History, and he taught it to every senior class. He also roamed the halls each day, checking in on classes. Often he would slip into one in progress.

"He could walk into a classroom so gently, so quietly," Stanley recalled, "that some of the students wouldn't know he was there. He'd stand in the back of the room so he was facing the teacher, not the students, just to see what was going on."

Williams was respected by the students at Chattahoochee High; and on the rare occasions he was forced to discipline, it took little more than his finger motioning the offender to his office to effect order.

"He was a great educator and a great man," Stanley said. "He taught the men's Sunday school class at the Baptist Church. The alumni association there is named for him. He made a big impact on the whole community."

By summer, teenage Stanley was eager to make money of his own. He got a job at the ice plant where he stood on the platform all day, handing off twenty-five to one-hundred pound ice blocks to customers who took them home to their iceboxes.

The next summer he landed a job at the newspaper office next door to his father's store. It was a weekly called the *Twin City News* and was owned by Spurgeon Dunn. The shop consisted of a four-page hand-fed press, a job press, a Linotype machine and larger type hand-set. Dunn needed shop help and was impressed that Stanley was a fast learner and was intrigued by every process. When school commenced in the fall, Stanley continued at the newspaper part-time.

"And since I was working at the newspaper," he said, "the school thought I should be the editor of the school paper, which was fine with me."

Now, Stanley endeavored to develop his writing skills in English class. The teacher was a strict middle-aged lady who, in addition to reading and writing, required her students to practice public speaking. Her technique was to call a student before the class and assign a topic about which the student had to speak extemporaneously in a convincing manner.

Stanley's incessant "umming" and "awwing" during his oration infuriated her. "She got so mad," he recalled, "that she picked up the glass inkwell on my desk and threw it at me. It hit the wall in back of me and busted. Fortunately it was empty. But that cured me from 'umming' and 'awwing,' I promise you that."

It was also during his senior year in high school that Stanley went on his first date. Bashful since childhood, it took some time for him to muster up nerve enough to ask Elise Scarborough if she would go out with him, but when he finally did she happily agreed. Stanley borrowed his father's truck, and the young couple drove to Marianna, Florida, where they nervously dined together and afterward saw a movie.

The date was a success, at least in Stanley's estimation, until the trip home. He recalled, "I was so timid in her presence that I let the pick-up run out of gas on us, and we had to hitch-hike back to Marianna to buy some fuel! But she was gracious about the whole thing."

By the time he graduated from high school in 1935, Stanley had an academic education as well as a practical one gained by his on-the-job experience. He remembered: "When I started work at the newspaper, I was so fascinated that I worked every hour I could. I just loved the work. I missed out on some of my high school education because I spent so much time at the newspaper. But I was learning something that became my life's vocation."

Graduation was not the only milestone to occur in Stanley's life at this time. An electric short set their house on fire during the same week. Parkman awoke in time to get everyone out, and they saved a few clothes and some pieces of furniture. As Stanley recalled the experience, "The only fire truck in the two towns was at Chattahoochee and, I believe, was manned by volunteers. So the house was utterly burned before it got there."

Homeless and without insurance, the Parkman's turned to family for help. Frances' aunt and uncle, Mr. and Mrs. Clyde Harbin, lived down the street in River Junction and offered to share their home with the displaced family. All moved into the Harbin home, except Stanley.

A railroad couple who lived across the street from the smoldering remains of his home offered him their upstairs attic. Stanley accepted. "There was no bath up there," he recalled, "so I had to go to the watering tub at our old cow barn and the place where we dressed the chickens. I'm not exaggerating! I got a good many of my baths out there." And he discovered that living in an attic wasn't always comfortable: "You talk about hot; it was hot up there beneath that tin roof!"

But Stanley would live there only a couple of months before another change in his life, and he would say his goodbyes to Elise Scarborough and River Junction both.

CHAPTER IX

MOVE TO MARIANNA

The rest of the world was preparing for war, and the U.S. economy was picking up some because we were making munitions and trucks and ships. I was pretty skilled at the printing trade by then, though I had not tried my hand at writing news. When the chance came, I took a new job in Marianna, Florida.

When The *Jackson County Floridian* needed a printer in the summer of 1935, John Winslett, the publisher, asked Spurgeon Dunn if he knew of one. Dunn said indeed he did, and Stanley was soon on the train headed for Marianna.

"For about a year I lived in a room at an old motel a block from the newspaper office," Stanley said. "They furnished room and board for guests and others, so I had all of my meals there in the dining room."

Others were also living at the motel. Stanley got to know a retired Superior Court Judge and a retired local businessman, both bachelors. Of them Stanley recalled: "They became pretty good buddies of mine, despite our age differences. I enjoyed being with them, and they with me."

Working at the *Jackson County Floridian,* enabled Stanley to hone his skills as an equipment operator. The military draft had begun, but he wasn't called up because newspaper work was considered semi-essential. Ironically, as more and more men were inducted, jobs became more plentiful in spite of the Depression.

Stanley moved his membership to the Marianna Baptist Church when he arrived and was soon ordained a deacon. And it was during his first year in Marianna that he met the woman who would become his wife.

In the summer of 1935, Frances Middlebrooke was living in Fort Worth, Texas, with her aunt and uncle. Her mother and father had divorced years before, and her re-married mother had died while Frances was still in high school. Frances' step-father managed a ten-cent store Marianna, Florida. After graduation, Frances came to Marianna to visit him and rented a room in the motel where Stanley was living.

"That's where we met," Stanley recalled. "She went to church with me a couple of times while she was there. I didn't have a vehicle, and so we never had what you'd call a serious date. What courtship we had was eating together at the motel and that kind of thing."

After two weeks, Frances returned to Fort Worth, but the courtship continued by telephone and letter. "We became engaged by mail, and I didn't see her again until she came back to Marianna for our wedding," said Stanley

The wedding took place at the Parkman's home in Chatta-hoochee. This was the first time Stanley's parents met Frances. It was also the first time Stanley had been home since moving to Marianna.

After the ceremony, John Winslett kindly lent the newly-weds his automobile to drive to Panama City Beach for a brief honeymoon. "We got married on Friday afternoon," Stanley said, "went down to Panama City, and came back Sunday afternoon. I had to be at work Monday morning."

The couple made their first home in a two-room, furnished apartment in a boarding house down the street from the newspaper office. The only household item they had to buy was a small toaster oven, which Frances used for cooking. A few months later they moved to a larger apartment on the opposite side of town. It was there that on June 23, 1938, David Stanley Parkman, III was born.

Shortly after this, the Advertising Manager at the newspaper was drafted, and his responsibilities fell to Stanley. His increase in pay wasn't much, but he appreciated the job and considered it "the beginning of my learning that part of the newspaper business."

By now it was two years since Frances had seen her father, who ran a furniture store in Fort Worth, or her aunt and uncle; and she was eager for them to get to know young David. Stanley was excited to show him off to relatives. He recalled, "David was a cute youngster if there ever was one, in my estimation anyway. And Frances was a master at dressing him."

Since they had no car, Stanley worried about how Frances would make the trip. However, the Marianna postmaster with whom he had become friends offered to drive them as far as New Orleans, where they could take a Greyhound the rest of the way. The responsibilities of Stanley's new advertising job didn't allow him to make the trip with Frances and David, but he rode with them as far as New Orleans.

About New Orleans, Stanley recalled, "It was the craziest place I'd ever seen in my life. During the evening we walked down Bourbon Street, and folks were craps shooting out on the sidewalk with the police standing right there watching them!"

It wasn't long until the war in Europe was in full swing. Stanley's job at the *Jackson County Floridian* became more and more demanding, and he was growing weary of the long hours and small pay. He discussed his situation with his former publisher Sturgeon Dunn and, with his encouragement and financial support, decided to start a competing newspaper, which he called *The Marianna Times*.

"Winslett didn't much like that I had done it," Stanley remembered. Getting started wasn't easy. "I had to buy used equipment—a Linotype machine and an old four-page hand-fed press, a paper cutter and hand type."

Stanley published the paper for a year without profit. Adding to his struggle was that printing help was in short supply due to the war effort. He recalled that the only employee he had was "an old drug addict who had done some work for the *Floridian*. He was a pretty good printer, but he couldn't operate a Linotype machine."

Frances lent a hand when she could, but she was expecting their second child, so her time was limited.

On May 29, 1941, Frances gave birth to Ralph Melvin Parkman. But the event was bittersweet. Stanley was sick with pneumonia, and all the money they had to show from the paper was $150.

Since he was laid up in bed, Stanley made out a deposit slip and asked the son of the addict working for him to take it to the bank. "Instead of doing that," Stanley said, "he left town with it!

At this dark moment, however, Stanley's father happened to stop by while on his chicken and egg route. He gave Stanley five dollars for groceries and some advice: shut down the newspaper and sell the equipment. As soon as he able, Stanley did so and used the proceeds to settle the bills.

In the meantime, Spurgeon Dunn heard of Stanley's predicament and got in touch with the owner and publisher of the paper in Quincy, the only other paper in Gadsden County, to see if he had a job opening. He did. So the Parkmans made preparations to move.

CHAPTER X

COMING TO QUINCY

> Nicolette had lost one or two people to the draft,
> so he gave me a job in Quincy selling advertising
> and doing some shop work. The place was similar
> to Marianna because they also did commercial
> printing jobs.

Before leaving Marianna, Stanley bought a used Model A
Ford despite the fact that rationing was in effect and gasoline
and tires were difficult to get. The family found a modest home
with a pasture out back for a cow, which Stanley bought to
furnish milk and butter.

It was now 1941, and he had been assigned a draft
number but had not been called. Along with other men in
the community, he joined the "Home Guard" to prepare for
probable induction in the army. "We didn't have guns to train
with," Stanley remembered, "but we practiced one night a
week with broom sticks under the direction of a retired army
officer."

Stanley's boss at the *Gadsden County Times* was C. C. Nicolette, who had bought the weekly paper as a hobby after
retiring from his position as a city editor at the *New York Times.*
Mr. Nicolette, recalled Stanley, "was an exceptional editor, but

he knew very little about advertising and shop work." What's more, he was an alcoholic and sipped straight bourbon all day. Stanley was amazed that this seemed to have no effect on his journalistic abilities. Eventually he considered him to be "as good an editorial writer as I have ever known."

The shop foreman and primary printer was Love Hutchison. Stanley helped him with some of the shop work but mainly sold advertising and did minor news writing.

The Parkmans soon joined the Quincy Baptist Church. Stanley was elected a deacon and later became the Sunday School Superintendent. He also served on the pulpit committee that called Dr. Henry Parker. Years later, after the Parkmans had moved to Carrollton, Dr. Parker served a term as President of the Florida Baptist Convention. Stanley was always proud to have had the opportunity to know and work with him.

Before the end of 1941 the news editor was drafted, and his duties became Stanley's. Soon after this, the *New York Times* persuaded Nicolette to return because their employees continued to be drafted, and they desperately needed him for the duration of the war.

Stanley recalled that, as a consequence, "I was virtually left in charge of the paper, and I was gaining valuable experience from all phases of its operations. In essence, it became my college education—the closest to one I ever got."

On December 7 of 1941 Stanley and all Americans experienced "the day that will live in infamy." Pearl Harbor was attacked by the Japanese. However, the people of Quincy were unaware of this momentous event until radio news reports the following day.

And if this were not enough concern, two weeks later, up in New York City, Mr. Nicolette suffered a fatal heart attack, leaving no will. Mrs. Nicolette, sadly, shared her husband's penchant for drink, and was wholly unable to provide any assistance with the newspaper. However, "Before Nicolette went back to New York," Stanley said, "he left a letter assigning the operation of the newspaper to those of us left behind, with me as chairman."

But since there was no will, the probate court had to settle Nicolette's estate. In the meantime, Stanley and Love Hutcheson worked ceaselessly to ensure that the paper continued publication. Stanley wrote all the news. Love handled the printing.

During this uneasy time, in addition to war reports a local death became big news. The superintendent of the state mental institution in Chattahoochee was found dead in his garage, apparently the victim of a self-inflicted gunshot wound.

Since the shooting had occurred on a Wednesday night, and the paper was printed on Thursday evening, Stanley had to decide how to report the story because the coroner had not officially announced it a suicide.

Stanley recalled, with a sigh, "I didn't have any better judgment than to carry it in the paper as a suicide. Well, I sweated over that one. The family threatened to sue, and I was the one in the hot seat. Fortunately, by Saturday the coroner had ruled it a suicide and that took the heat off of me."

Life in Quincy continued under the war-imposed circumstances. On October 25, 1942, Frances gave birth to their third child, a daughter they named Patricia Ann. Meanwhile, in the final settlement of the Nicolette estate, the courts were selling the newspaper. Stanley lamented the fact that he had no money to buy it. Eventually, the *Gadsden County Times* was sold at auction to the highest bidder, a tobacco packing house owner who was running for state senator.

"He didn't know a thing about the newspaper business," said Stanley, "but he wanted an advertising vehicle for his campaign and directed me to make that of it, because I was pretty much still in charge." But such unreasonable conditions were not agreeable to Stanley, and he began to look for new employment.

CHAPTER XI

GEORGIA BOUND

I found two ads in *The Publisher's Auxiliary*, a national publication for small newspapers, that interested me because they were fairly close by–Carrollton, Georgia, and Athens, Tennessee. By this time we had our first automobile, but gasoline and tires were rationed, so I traveled by bus.

In September of 1944 Stanley Parkman boarded a Greyhound for Carrollton, Georgia. When he arrived in the quaint college town, he met with Clyde Tuttle, owner and operator of the *Times Free Press*, the only newspaper. After the meeting, he went on Athens, Tennessee, and spoke with the publisher of the newspaper there. After considering both opportunities, he decided that the one in Carrollton was better for him and his family.

Stanley recalled, "Before the war there had been two newspapers in Carrollton, *The Carroll County Times*, owned by the Thomason family, and *The Carrollton Free Press*, owned by the Meeks family. The Thomasons also ran a successful commercial printing business, so early in the war they sold the *Times* to a new-comer named Passifant. He managed to persuade the Meeks family to sell him their paper as well, thus eliminating any competition. The combined paper became known as the *Times-Free Press*. It changed hands several times over the next few years and eventually was owned by Tuttle.

"Tuttle knew nothing about weekly newspapers when he bought the paper," said Stanley. "He had been a small magazine publisher up in North Carolina, so that was my first indication that I might have made the wrong decision."

Nevertheless, two weeks later Stanley brought Frances and the children to Carrollton. He hadn't been able to find a house for them, so they joined him in the Carrollton Hotel where he was staying.

Stanley vividly remembered the day the moving van with their belongings arrived, and they had no place for them. "But M.L. Fisher had his hardware store on the ground floor of a building on Newnan Street, and he permitted us to unload our furniture into the upstairs space," he said.

The hotel staff welcomed the young family with open arms. Their first day in Carrollton was October 24, which was daughter Patti's second birthday. In a gesture of kindness, the hotel staff presented her with a birthday cake with two blazing candles during lunch.

Despite the warm hospitality shown them, a hotel was no place for three small children. They still could not find a house, so they decided that Frances and the children would go to Birmingham, Alabama, and stay with her aunt.

Eventually, Stanley found something suitable, two rooms for rent in a downtown house owned by a couple who didn't need the space. They would share the bath.

The family was reunited. Stanley recalls, with a smile: "David had started first grade before leaving Quincy and was then enrolled in Birmingham. In December, he started school in Carrollton. He was in the first grade in three different states. We've often wondered how he ever passed!"

The family joined the First Baptist Church, and started a new routine. Stanley became involved in establishing the city recreation department and was put on the Board of Directors.

All was going smoothly. It wasn't long, however, before he would discover that things at the newspaper weren't what they had seemed.

"When I came," he said, "Tuttle was down to one person in the print shop, and the newspaper was in a low state of affairs. Tuttle's bad management and his lack of know-how hurt; also, war rationing was so strict that merchants didn't need to do much advertising. At that young age I didn't have better sense to find out this

before I got here."

Furthermore, Tuttle had a habit of lambasting local merchants in his front-page column for not supporting the newspaper. Businessmen and citizens alike began to resent him, and Stanley soon was certain he had made a mistake in taking the job: "It was a bad situation, and I regretted that I had not taken the Athens job. I contacted them, and they said they still needed help. I remember thinking I should have just gone there to start with."

But the Parkman's had gained allies during their short time in Carrollton, especially in the church, and fate was about to play a huge role in their lives.

CHAPTER XII

BIRTH OF A NEWSPAPER

Unbeknownst to me, M.C. Roop, T.J. Lawler, Tom Loftin, and Dr. Reese, all of whom I knew from the First Baptist Church, had had a meeting or two, led by Roop and Lawler. They came to the conclusion they'd had enough of Tuttle and his newspaper. For the good of the town they wanted to organize another locally owned newspaper, one that would have a positive outlook on the community.

After nearly a year struggling under Tuttle at the *Times-Free Press*, Stanley was prepared to move his family to Tennessee. It was 1945, the war was coming to an end, and there had been no improvement at the paper. Thirty years old and unsure of his future, Stanley was very interested when M.C. Roop and T.J. Lawler approached him with a plan that would put him in charge of his own newspaper.

"They asked me how much I thought it would take to start a paper," he said. "I told them I thought we could do it with $10,000. Well, I was not thinking that out of that money I was going to have to meet a payroll for at least a month, rent a building, and pay for the equipment and the expense of setting it up."

But he had specified his figure, and the proposal was hastily put into action. One-hundred dollar shares were sold, with the provisions that no individual could buy more than a $500 interest, and that when he was able, Stanley would have the option of buying the other's shares. Stanley borrowed the money for his $500 share from his father. The stock sold well, but the offering raised $400 less than the $10,000 goal.

Stanley got to work buying and installing the necessary machinery and equipment. As agreed, he paid himself a salary of $75 per week, the same as he'd made with Tuttle. He rented a small, two-story building located on the alley between Groover-Smith's Furniture Store and The Farmers Store. In nearby Newnan he bought a linotype machine from an out-of-business print shop, bringing it to Carrollton in a borrowed truck with the aid of a high school student.

"That thing weighed 2000 pounds or more," he recalled. "We borrowed some skids and rolled it onto the truck. Then we came back up here and Mr. Bill Traylor, who ran The Farmer's Store let me borrow his skids, bless his heart. By the time we got it unloaded, it was pouring down rain. When I came back the next morning, the floor was four-inches deep in water, and part of the Linotype machine we'd just bought was under water. It would have discouraged anybody who had any sense."

True to his nature, immediately after discovering that Stanley was in the process of starting a competing paper, Tuttle turned his venom on him. Every new day brought another criticism of Parkman-and-Company in front-page Tuttle fashion.

However, publicity being publicity, the ploy backfired and succeeded in piquing the interest of Carrollton citizens in the upcoming paper. That, coupled with the clever idea of having soldiers just home from the war sell subscriptions house to house brought the number of pre-paid subscriptions to 2000 before a single issue was printed.

"I gave the vets half of the three dollar yearly subscription as commission, and they sold them like hotcakes," he said." I think people were sympathetic about them coming back from the war and were more than willing to buy from them."

One problem Stanley encountered was getting shop help. The only person he could find was Charlie Williamson, who was long retired from the Thomason' operation. He agreed to run the Linotype on a part-time basis. The rest of the work at the new newspaper would be up to Stanley. Even though Frances was a housewife with three children, she helped by writing the Society News and sold advertising when she could.

Stanley bought the other pieces of equipment that were needed: a four-page handfed, printing press, a casting box for molten metal used for casting cardboard mats, a metal saw for trimming and shaping type slugs and illustrations, cases to hold larger size type, and a machine to fold the printed sheets of newspaper. The expenses were such that sacrifices were necessary. Coca-Cola crates served as both tables and chairs. Stanley handfed the press for hours, printing enough copies for every postal patron in the county to receive the first month's paper.

It was under these conditions that on November 8, 1945— six days after the end of World War II—the first issue of *The Carroll County Georgian* was published. The following statement by Stanley appeared prominently:

POLICY OF THE GEORGIAN

A definite and honest statement of the policy of a new newspaper publication is expected by the general public and its potential readers. That is only natural and the sensible thing to do.

For that reason and for the purpose of answering important questions that might already be framed in the minds of the people of Carroll County, The Carroll County Georgian, in its first issue, takes pleasure in giving a factual outline of its editorial policy and ideals upon which it was founded.

The motto of the national organization of Rotary and all its affiliated clubs is: "He profits most who serves best." Jesus used about the same motto, only in different words, and many of the most successful business men of all ages have found that such an ideal is good. We believe the saying is true and with that in mind the Georgian is launched.

By way of service to the people of Carroll County this newspaper will be strictly independent, progressive, and seek to foster a definite program of improvement and progress within the limits of the wealth produced by the people who make this their home.

We have a deep conviction that the county of Carroll and the city of Carrollton are now at the threshold of their greatest era of prosperity. Our people have taken the war in their stride, contributed their share in men and materials, and are now eagerly entering the years of peace with a confidence that is born of knowledge that this land is great.

The faith in this county of the men who have an interest in this newspaper was the reason for its founding. Our platform for the immediate future is: better roads for all sections; better schools in a more adequate educational system; fair distribution of the tax burden and sufficient revenue for city and county to meet the needs; intensify program of conservation for our natural resources; diversification of our farming to provide greater agricultural income and a job for every returning service man or woman from Carroll County.

This paper harbors no ill will for a single individual or group in the county. In the words of someone else, "We ain't mad with nobody." We respect the right of every man to his own opinion and we will sincerely try to always give substantial reasons for opinions we express. We have no political ambitions and will as nearly as reasonably possible maintain a neutral attitude in local and state politics. By neutral attitude we mean that a true picture of all issues and candidates will be diligently sought.

We guarantee that any person in Carroll County has use of a suitable space in this paper for

the publication of his views regarding the administration of city and county affairs or regarding the policy and statements in this newspaper, providing, of course, that such views and statements are not libelous, are reasonably brief, and are signed.

The Georgian is financially strong. That statement is made so that the people might know that we are in a position to carry out our pledge of service to the county without the restraints of limited finances. We intend to remain financially strong, and for that reason expect to make a reasonable profit from the service we render.

We recognize that the duty of any good and ethical newspaper is to present the news, all the news, in a truthful manner, and to as nearly as humanly possible interpret the events editorially to provoke the thoughts and actions of the people served. If those things are done in a creditable manner, it follows that the business interests of the area will want to publish their messages to the readers of the newspaper.

This paper will make mistakes. It probably has made some of them in this first issue and it will be strange indeed if it does not make them again. The best way we know of correcting those mistakes and knowing our faults is to keep an open and clear mind receptive to the criticisms and suggestions of our friends, and to seek to do a better job of service with each succeeding issue.

We expect to be in business a great many years carrying out this policy to the advantage of our people.

CHAPTER XIII

GAINING GROUND

Immediately following the war there were few jobs for men in Carroll County. Most of the workers were women in the textile mills. So one of our first objectives was to bring jobs for men to the area.

By the end of 1945 the war was over, and returning soldiers were desperate for employment. One of them, a young man by the name of John Camp, approached Stanley about helping out in the shop. Stanley recalled, "He didn't have any experience in printing, but he was young and strong, and I hired him to help with the installation of equipment and so forth." But Camp was eager to learn, and by the time of the second issue he was feeding the press, thus freeing Stanley for other tasks. Advertising was Stanley's most pressing issue, but rationing still made sales difficult. However, from the first issue on, several local businessmen were happy to advertise in the new paper.

"Tom Loftin at the hardware store supported us with advertising," said Stanley, "and Ed Copeland at the grocery store and Mr. Glen Holmes with his Dodge automobile dealership. But it was still a very difficult time."

In spite of hardships, the *Georgian* continued gaining ground while Tuttle and the *Times-Free Press* continued to lose. Tuttle stepped up his efforts to discredit both Stanley and what he referred to as his "brand new baby" by adding offensive cartoons to his already seedy column. He even assigned nicknames to Stanley and his stockholders; "Deacon Parkman" and "Fish-Face Loftin," among them.

Stanley refrained from responding to Tuttle's antics. In fact, he never made mention of Tuttle or the *Times* in his paper at all. "We didn't do editorial criticism of anything or anyone," he expained. "My policy and practice was to be upbeat and positive and encouraging of everything that was trying to get started in those years after the war."

The *Georgian* continued its effort to bring in new industry with regular praise of the county and its resources. In fact, Stanley had become so enamored with Carrollton that when the Parkman's fourth child, a daughter, was born on November 16, 1945, she was given the name Carroll Ann in honor of the family's beloved new home. Delivered by Dr. Steve Worthy at the Carrollton Clinic, Carroll was the last of Stanley and Frances' children.

Not long after Carroll's birth, two gentlemen called on Stanley at the newspaper office and said they wished to discuss business conditions in the Carrollton area. "I didn't know who they were," recalled Stanley, "and they showed up unannounced. But we were always looking for new businesses in town, so I was boosting Carrollton to beat the band. Well, it wasn't until later that day that I found out they were there to buy the *Times* from Tuttle!"

And shortly they did. The buyers were Jewel Dean and his business associate from Ohio. With Tuttle gone, the two began their endeavor to rebuild the tattered *Times-Free Press.* Dean's business associate, however, perhaps recognizing an uphill battle, returned to Ohio after only a few months, leaving Dean without help in his struggle with the *Georgian.*

It was a struggle that the *Georgian* won because of events that occurred two years after the paper began, when it became eligible for a second-class mailing permit. The lower postal rate drastically reduced operating expenses. In addition, the *Georgian* was also eligible to carry legal advertising, which was awarded by the clerk of court, the sheriff, and the probate judge. Stanley recalled, "The three county officers gave their advertising to us, primarily because we had more circulation than the *Times-Free Press* by that time."

Stanley was now qualified to join the Georgia Press Associ- ation. Founded in 1887, the association is comprised of participating newspapers throughout the state, from small rural weeklies to large urban dailies, the *Atlanta Journal and Constitution* being the largest. The first GPA convention Stanley attended was in 1948 in Savannah. At the convention the next year, Stanley had an interesting experience. Nominations for president of the association had just been opened when Gene Methwin, a newspaper man from Vidalia, Georgia, hobbled into the hall on crutches; He was still recovering from wounds he sustained in the war for which he had been awarded the Purple Heart. A voice from the crowd called out, "I nominate Gene Methwin."

"I was so moved by the gesture that before I really thought about it, I seconded the motion," said Stanley. "And Gene Methwin was elected president almost unanimously."

The president of the association was responsible for naming the Board of Directors, who were from various congressional districts and served rotating three-year terms. The year after Methwin was elected, Stanley was surprised to be named a Director. "That was only the second convention I had attended," he said, "and being named a director was a big boost to the *Georgian*."

During the same convention, Stanley entered the *Georgian* in the competition for best newspaper in a circulation category and won the General excellence Award.

Meanwhile, in Carrollton, the Chamber of Commerce was organized with the *Georgian* playing a large part in drumming up interest. The county began a cooperative community dairy operation similar to a successful one in Alabama. A sales barn was built to support local livestock sales, and rural electricity made its debut.

Stanley recalled, with excitement in his voice, "Mr. Bob Tisinger was a great moving force in that. He went down and sat on the porch of the Little White House with Franklin D. Roosevelt and set up the founding basis of the Rural Electric Association. Under that impetus, Carroll County began to thrive."

The community benefited again when Bill Lomason put up $100,000 to build the county's first library, the balance for which was raised in the community and also provided through federal funds.

Then, Mr. C.M. Tanner donated $100,000 to found Tanner Memorial Hospital. More good news was that the job market was growing by leaps and bounds.

It seemed that Carroll County, the city of Carrollton, and the *Carroll County Georgian* were on the right road.

CHAPTER XIV

TO TAKE A CHANCE

A fellow from Texas approached me about putting on a circulation campaign. He had heard about the progress we had made and that I was an officer of the Georgia Press Association in line to become its president. He had held campaigns in Oklahoma and Texas but not in Georgia. I was afraid to do it, but he managed to persuade me.

In 1953, the circulation of the *Carroll County Georgian* was steadily rising, but Stanley did not have enough funds to buy out his shareholders. When he heard that he might be able to raise money through a contest he was skeptical.

The premise of the contest was simple: people who entered would be paid a commission on each subscription sold. The one who sold the most would win a new Buick. Second prize was $1,000 in cash. Stanley saw this as a lot to risk. In addition, newsprint was still rationed. Even if the contestants sold enough subscriptions to cover costs, there was no guarantee he could find enough paper to print so many copies.

But the smooth-talking Texan had no doubt that the success of the *Georgian* would open doors for other such projects in Georgia. His wife came to Carrollton to oversee the operation.

After much thought, Stanley decided to take the chance.

"The first thing they did," he remembered, "was put that new car from Billy Morrow's Buick place up on the square, and I had to pay for it! I was worried we wouldn't bring in enough money."

By the end of February fifteen people had entered the contest.

He remembered, "The contest started in February of 1953, and the weather was really cold. "As the days passed, the thing caught on," said Stanley, and "we could barely keep up with it. It ran until the end of March. I was literally amazed. They had sold enough subscriptions and renewals to pay for the new car, the cost of putting on the campaign, all the cash prizes, and left me with $10,000 in the bank!"

Now Stanley was financially able to buy out the other stockholders. But there were problems. Dr. L. C. Roberts had died, leaving his share to his son, attorney Oscar Roberts. M. C. Roop reneged on his promise to sell his shares to Stanley, and in the interim had also passed away. Oscar Roberts was the attorney for his estate, and he managed to take control of Roop's stock as well, the two interests equaling ten percent. Like Roop, Roberts was unwilling to sell. Their shares were the only ones Stanley was not able to acquire.

Though he did not own the paper outright, Stanley now had controlling interest in the paper he had almost single-handedly made a success. He realized that his chance-taking had been justified.

CHAPTER XV

THE OPPOSITION

During that time, Jewel Dean and I had several long talks. We'd get in the car and drive out on back roads so folks in town wouldn't see us. He was anxious to find a way we could combine the two papers and stop the bleeding of his finances. But I couldn't find one because he had so many debts we'd have to pay off in the process.

In 1953, Sam Boykin was up for reelection as Superior Court Judge in the Coweta Circuit of which Carroll County was a part. He was the youngest of three Boykin brothers, all of whom were tenacious and tremendously successful lawyers. They had managed to monopolize most of the legal business in Carrollton, so the popular view was that they controlled the town. Consequently, "A lot of folks didn't like them," said Stanley, "like Roy Richards and Lynn Holmes, who wanted power, too."

In 1950 Richards had founded Southwire Company, a wire and cable manufacturer that supplied much of the wire for the REA mission to bring electricity to the South. He was Chairman of the Board of the People's Bank. He also chaired the Hospital

Authority that managed the newly built Tanner Medical Center and encouraged community involvement on its behalf.

Holmes owned and operated a Western Auto Store and plumbing supply company and was a director of West Georgia National Bank.

The *Georgian* editorially endorsed Sam Boykin for reelection. But Boykin's opposition was a lawyer from LaGrange who had joined forces with those in the Carrollton community who were against the Boykin-brother cartel.

Boykin was reelected. But Stanley learned a valuable lesson:

Never endorse *any* candidate. "I lost quite a bit of advertising from local businessmen," he said, "who didn't particularly like the outcome of that election."

Jewel Dean saw the discord as his opportunity to revive the fast-dying *Times-Free Press.* His first move was to borrow $10,000 from Roy Richards' People's Bank. He got another $10,000 from West Georgia National Bank on Lynn Holmes' say-so.

In the meantime, Stanley needed more space for the *Georgian.* He rented a building across the alley from the current location and moved the paper. He soon realized that the large increase in subscribers caused by the circulation contest necessitated a faster printing press.

He located a used Goss 8-page rotary press in a Midwestern state. It used rolls of paper instead of sheets, eliminating the need for someone to feed it, and printed both sides of the page at once. In addition, it automatically folded the freshly-printed sheets and ran 2500 copies of an 8-page section per hour as opposed to 1000 an hour with the old press.

"They wanted about $8,000 for it," said Stanley. "It was a lot of money at that time, but we desperately needed it."

West Georgia National Bank had begun in competition to the People's Bank only a few years before, and several of the *Georgian's* original stockholders also held stock in the bank. Since Roop, Lawler, and Holmes were directors, Stanley was confident West Georgia would loan him the money for the new press.

However, neither bank would. Stanley said, "They had a tight-fisted view of new businesses, and we were in competition with the *Times* to whom they had already loaned money."

But Stanley was not daunted. Knowing that the C&S Bank of Savannah had opened a branch in Atlanta, he called the chairman and told him who he was and why he needed a loan to buy a new press. "He never even asked me why I didn't borrow it from the local banks," Stanley recalled. "In that five minute telephone conversation he told me yes, that I could borrow the money." The chairman gave him the name and number of a man at the Atlanta branch, and by the end of the month the Goss press was printing twice as many copies of the *Carroll County Georgian* as before.

CHAPTER XVI

THE MERGER

A fellow who owned papers in Cedartown, Gadsden, Alabama, LaGrange, and two or three other towns, got the idea he'd buy both Carrollton papers and consolidate them. He talked to Dean first, but Dean couldn't make a deal because of his debts. Well, the man didn't want to buy one paper without buying the other. But I wasn't selling.

By the fall of 1954, Dean had been unable to pay even the interest on the money he had borrowed from the two banks. Richards and Holmes, endorsers of the respective notes, realized that they were responsible if Dean didn't pay. So the two hatched a plan and bought Dean's interest in the *Times-Free Press,* much to the delight of Dean, who promptly retired to Florida.

They found a newspaper man in Kentucky named Startsman and brought him to Carrollton to revamp the *Times.* Richards instructed his personal secretary at Southwire to take charge of ingratiating Startsman with the people of Carrollton, and she took the newcomer to civic club meetings and other activities around town.

Smiling, Stanley recalled, "Mr. Startsman went home to spend Christmas with his family and never came back. I think he realized he was on an uphill jog!"

Left with no one to run the newspaper, Richards and Holmes began a campaign to persuade Stanley to merge the two papers.

"I'll never forget Roy Richards calling me to come out to his office at Southwire to sit down and talk," said Stanley. "'Now Stanley,' he said, 'this town just can't support two newspapers. And I can't keep putting money into it, because I can't take it from Southwire. But if you won't merge the papers, I won't have any choice but to do exactly that.'"

Stanley knew that without a Southwire of his own to draw money from he would not be able to compete with Richards and Holmes' paper. It was for this reason he agreed to merge the *Carroll County Georgian* and the *Times-Free Press* in June of 1955.

The equipment from the *Times* was sold, and Richards and Holmes each put in the additional funds needed to acquire the forty-five percent interest that Stanley already had in the merger. Since Oscar Roberts refused to sell his ten percent to either party, no investor had controlling interest in the operation

Because the *Times* ran two issues a week and the *Georgian* ran three, the new Tuesday paper became the *Times-Free Press,* the Thursday paper the *Carroll County Georgian,* and the Saturday paper, simply, *Saturday.*

CHAPTER XVII

THE GLORY YEARS

At this time a labor union was trying to organize Southwire. I fought against the union in favor of Southwire, and Roy Richards was appreciative. I had some tough discourses with organizers because I carried ads in the paper asking Southwire employees not to support the union's organizing efforts.

The mid fifties served as a turning point in the success of the newspaper, and Stanley was able to breathe easy for the first time since coming to Carrollton.

He fought hard to bring more industry to the area and to keep the labor union out of Southwire. He had continued to be active in the Georgia Press Association, attending every convention since he joined. And in 1954 he was elected its president. He had joined the Rotary Club in 1948 and, coincidentally, was nominated by Shirley Boykin, the middle of the Boykin brothers, to become president the same year.

Boykin had served as the Rotary's president the previous year, and the nominating committee was composed of all past club presidents, the most recent serving as chairman. "Being president of the GPA was a big job in itself," Stanley said.

"So I explained to Shirley my situation and asked if they could wait until the following year to nominate me. Well, he quickly explained to me in no uncertain terms that when you are nominated for President of the Rotary Club, you serve as President of the Rotary Club. And that was that. So I served as president of both the Rotary Club and the Georgia Press Association the very same year." In fact, when the first issue of the merged paper was printed, Stanley was in Savannah presiding over the Georgia Press Association's annual convention.

When he returned a few days later, he resumed the fight against the unionization of Southwire. The attorney representing the union visited him with a group of organizers and asked to buy a full-page ad in the paper explaining union policy. Stanley told the attorney he wouldn't do so. "And you talk about some hot words," Stanley recalled. "He told me I had a constitutional responsibility as a legitimate newspaper to carry his ad, but after a long hour he realized he couldn't force me to."

Stanley did accept an invitation to attend a union meeting at a church in the south part of the county to reveal the reasons he opposed unionization. A young news editor fresh out of the University of Georgia journalism school, whom he had recently hired, offered to follow him to the church.

Stanley recalled that at the meeting, "I was talking under very adverse circumstances, trying to let them know that due to the economy, the added expense of unions would destroy existing jobs and throw people out of work. But every time I tried to make a point, somebody jumped up to argue with me. Well, while I was in the church, somebody slipped out and cut the tires on my car." Luckily, no one cut his young companion's, and he was able to drive Stanley back to town.

Stanley's efforts played a part in the Southwire employee's vote against unionization, and he moved on to other newspaper matters.

CHAPTER XVIII

BUILDING AN ORGANIZATION

> An interesting fact about buying the papers that
> we did, and a fact that I am right proud of, is I
> never went out trying to buy any of them. The
> owners always came to me. We were already
> printing several of them because we had a fast
> press.

By 1955, the *Georgian* shop was printing several newspapers
in the surrounding area because its newer press was faster
and therefore more cost-efficient than the older models in
other shops. One of those was the *Villa Rican,* owned by Robby
Robinson, and at the time the only other paper in Carroll
County. When Robinson contacted Stanley one day and asked
him to buy the paper, Stanley obliged.

"We maintained the office there," said Stanley, "and, of
course, all the news writing and advertising sales were done
by that staff. The only thing we did in Carrollton was the
mechanical side."

Kate Golden, owner and operator of the nearby *Bowdon
Bulletin,* asked Stanley to print her issues. Later, Golden
developed Alzheimer's disease and became unable to continue.
When she passed away, Stanley recalled, "I got her paper out

for her for several weeks until her two brothers who were settling her estate came and asked us to buy the paper. So we did."

The *Buchanan Tribune* was another paper that joined Stanley's growing organization. Though exceptionally small, the *Tribune* was essential because Buchanan was the seat of neighboring Haralson County. The owner was an elderly gentleman close to death when he contacted Stanley about his wish to sell. After purchasing it, Stanley closed down its full-time office and began printing the paper in Carrollton. He realized, however, that he needed a part-time employee in Buchanan to handle advertising, subscriptions, and news items. He hired Janet Ayers, a senior at Buchanan High School.

"They had a program where she'd go to classes in the morning and work in the afternoon," recalled Stanley. "I didn't know much about her until she became President of Carroll Technical College. She did! Years later she reminded me that her first job was working for me at the *Buchanan Tribune*."

By Christmas Eve of 1955, Stanley-and-Company owned four newspapers in the surrounding area. While working in his office that day, Stanley received a call from "Hoss" Meeks, owner of the *Bremen Gateway*, who, well into his nineties, felt it was as good a time as any to sell his paper and retire.

"I told him sure, that I'd be glad to talk to him about it after Christmas was over. But he said he didn't want to wait until then, he wanted to sell it *that* day," Stanley recalled.

By noontime Christmas Eve, the organization had grown to five.

The *Gateway* was followed soon after by the Fairburn newspaper that was owned by a lawyer and his wife who viewed it as little more than a hobby. After her husband passed away, the wife asked Stanley to buy the paper. "We were already printing it for them," said Stanley, "and it was more than she wanted to keep up. So we bought it, too."

The *Tallapoosa Journal* was owned and operated by Ralph and Frances Green. They had struggled for years to publish the paper themselves, but upon Ralph's death, Frances gave Stanley the opportunity to buy it. He did so, and Frances continued to edit the paper until her health forced her to retire a few years later.

It was also around this time that an Atlanta radio man named Boling Brannon paid Stanley a visit. Brannon had bought the *Douglas County Sentinel* but was displeased with its progress. He asked Stanley to take on the responsibility of printing it.

Stanley agreed. But soon Brannon was also in financial trouble, and tried to persuade Stanley to loan him $25,000 dollars to save his paper. "I told him I was sorry but we're not in the banking business," Stanley said. "Not more than two weeks later he came back and said that he'd just sell the whole thing to me for twenty-five thousand."

Stanley and his directors decided it was an offer they couldn't refuse. When the deal was sealed, they kept a staff of two to run the Douglasville office and continued printing the *Sentinel* in Carrollton. The editor and advertising manager would bring the news copy to Carrollton for printing, and then carry the finished product back to Douglasville for distribution.

"After a while," said Stanley, "those two guys got the notion they wanted to start a competing paper in Douglas County. They came into my office one Wednesday and told me their plans. This was the first I had heard of it!"

The duo offered to take the *Sentinel* to the post office for distribution one last time, but Stanley declined. "By that time I was upset, and I said, 'No, I think I want you to just give me the key, and we'll take the paper to the post office and lock up the office.'"

Now Stanley was left with the problem of getting out the next week's paper. Jay Horton, the advertising director at Carrollton, had found Bruce Thomas, whom he had worked with in Alabama, to run the *Bremen Gateway* when it was purchased. Stanley turned to Thomas to be responsible for the Douglasville paper. Thomas said yes, he'd be there the next morning. He was joined by Tommy Toles, who had been the editor of the Fairburn paper. The following week, the *Sentinel* went out with a whopping twenty-four pages, twice what it had ever been before.

"Bruce and Tommy just blew them off the road," Stanley exclaimed. "I don't know what became of those other guys. They never did start a new paper."

The most interesting acquisition was that of the *Manchester Mercury.* The owner Ralph Rice had two facilities: a fairly large commercial printing plant and the newspaper plant.

Though the *Mercury* was a successful business, Rice suffered from a heart condition that eventually required surgery. During that time, and unsure of his prognosis, Rice decided to sell the newspaper, keeping only the commercial printing plant. The *Gadsden Alabama Times,* which owned a chain of papers including those in LaGrange and Cedartown, bought the *Mercury* from him and continued to run it successfully.

Eventually, though, Rice recovered from his operation and wanted to get back in the newspaper business. However, the sales agreement with *Gadsden* contained a stipulation that he could not enter into competition with the *Mercury* for a period of ten years.

Stanley said, "He was still healthy when the ten years ran out, so he started another paper, the *Star,* printing it in his shop. It was a fancy weekly newspaper, done on that slick commercial paper.

The owners of the *Mercury* were chagrined. Rice offered to end their competition by buying back his former paper or selling his new one to them. But they couldn't reach an agreement.

"One Sunday afternoon the fellow from Gadsden paid me a visit at home," said Stanley. "I wasn't there, so he pinned a note to the door, saying, 'Stanley, you probably don't know about this, but Ralph Rice and I are serious competitors in Manchester. I won't sell to him and he won't sell to me. But I'll sell *you* the *Mercury*, and I believe Ralph will sell you the *Star.'*"

Within a week, Stanley purchased both the *Manchester Mercury* and the *Manchester Star.* He had not been to Manchester before the transactions; and when he went to inspect what he had bought, he discovered that Bob Tribble, who had been running the *Mercury*, had just been released from the hospital. "He'd had some kind of serious illness, and so the paper was in a struggle," Stanley said.

And to worsen matters, Tribble had not been informed that his job was no longer necessary. "I didn't need two crews," said Stanley. "The man from Gadsden had said he was taking Tribble to be his advertising manager, but Tribble didn't know anything about it."

Bob Tribble had run a service station for a living before being hired by the *Mercury*. Upon realizing that he was without employment, he responded to a sales ad for a small newspaper in Woodbury whose owners were retiring. Stanley observed, "Well, low and behold, Tribble started buying up newspapers just like I was doing. He bought the Woodbury paper, and then he bought the Hogansville

paper, and then he bought and installed the printing equipment to print them in Manchester, where he still lived. First thing you know, he had about six of these small weekly newspapers in the surrounding counties."

Several years later, on yet another Christmas Eve morning, Stanley received a call in his office in Carrollton from Tribble. Stanley recalls that he said: 'Stanley, I know you're having a pretty hard time coming down here to Manchester once a week to see about your paper, so I'd just like to buy it from you to add to my organization."

Stanley was surprised. He asked Tribble what kind of payment arrangement he had in mind, and Tribble responded that he had a check for half the purchase price in his hand. "He said he'd give me the check today and pay the rest by the month over the next two years," Stanley recalled. That afternoon, Tribble came to Carrollton with the check, and Stanley handed over ownership of the paper to him.

"He started with that kind of pace," Stanley recalled, "and as of last year [2004] he owned twenty-three newspapers. He's still going strong." Stanley chuckled. "He's a multi-millionaire, and he's not running a service station anymore."

CHAPTER XIX

LIVING A DREAM

After 1950 the paper just took off. Our competition was doing worse and worse. Then we merged the papers in '55, and I can't say anything but that things were like a flower garden for me from then on.

The *Georgian* and the newly acquired weeklies were doing very well. Frances enjoyed Social News writing and was a peerless proofreader. Stanley continued his editorials and took pride in the growing organization.

It seemed that in no time the Parkman children were young adults. David, now in high school, seemed to be following in the footsteps of his father. "He played center for the Trojans in high school," said Stanley, "and he began to write sports news for the paper." When he graduated, David enrolled at the local college. Two years later he transferred to the University of Georgia where he studied Journalism, to his father's delight.

Speaking fondly, Stanley recalled, "David had always been interested in writing, and they made him editor of the university paper, the *Red and Black*. That was a great accomplishment in my estimation."

David's editorship followed by a couple of years that of another Carrolltonian with ties to the Parkmans. Tracy Stallings, who in later years would become a vice-president at the local college, the city Mayor, and a Representative in the Georgia House, began his journalism career as a sportswriter for Stanley while still in high school.

Of his days at the *Georgian,* Stallings said, "Stanley gave me a job writing sports news before I could even type. I wrote everything out by hand and took it to the newspaper office to be typed up." Stallings continued working for the paper through his high school and college years, during which time he became very close to Stanley. In fact, because his own father had died when he was eleven, Stallings considered Stanley a father-figure and credited much of his writing ability to him.

When Stallings became editor of the *Red and Black,* Stanley published the following editorial in the *Georgian:*

THE RED AND BLACK NEEDED A MAN

It's rather interesting to notice how things seem to mold together and work out the way they do.

For example that story that developed over the past few weeks regarding the Red and Black, the University of Georgia newspaper.

It all started with a rather fiery young fellow, serving as editor of the student newspaper, writing an editorial calling for admission of Negro students to the University. Then came the next chapter which was the reply of Roy Harris, state political leader and member of the Board of Regents. Mr. Harris, in a rather violent temper told the editor that such writing as that would stop or the Board of Regents would withdraw their financial support of the newspaper.

Here were two lines of thought that could not be brought together and Mr. Harris, holding the whip hand, won his point. Winning his point meant the establishment of a faculty commission that will have some type of supervision over controversial writings in the paper. It also meant that the editor and some of his staff members resigned.

I asked some people who know the answer, how the student body of the University felt about the matter. The answer was that a majority of the student body probably would not go along with the editor on his idea of admission of Negro students at the present time, but they would solidly back him in his right to say what he wanted to in the paper. Man, that thrilled my old journalistic heart. Maybe they won't agree with what he says but they will fight for his right to say it.

Now back to what I started out to say, with these background facts in mind.

Last week, the time came to elect an editor for the Red and Black for the next quarter and along with him the remainder of the staff.

With this very trying situation confronting the Board that selects the editor, they could not select just any journalism student who maybe happened to be popular or who stood well in campus politics. This time they had to select a MAN!

Tracy Stallings, of Carrollton, was the unanimous choice as editor and Alvin Shackleford, of Carrollton, was the unanimous choice as business manager.

I don't care where they might have looked; they would not have found a better combination to meet the needs of the hour for the historic Red and Black. Some other time somebody else would have been alright but this was a time of crisis and Tracy Stallings was there.

Am I not just being prejudiced and a little sentimental, you ask? No, I am not. I have been close to this young man, probably closer than anyone outside his immediate family, since he was a sophomore in Carrollton High School and started working with the Georgian after school and during vacations. He has what it takes to do the job.

His task will not be simple. He will be closely watched by Roy Harris and other political tyrants who would throttle the voice of anyone not agreeing with them, if they could. Tracy will also be watched as closely by those radicals who thrive on dissention and turmoil.

> I think he will be a disappointment to both groups. Unless I miss my guess, he will live up to the standards of that great majority of freedom-loving, God-fearing Americans who know how to stay in the middle of the road. Tracy and Alvin and the other staff members will have no need for fear of oppression because they will be supported by the vast majority who will fight for their right to say and write what they like.
>
> Incidentally, Lucrete Marshall, our news editor had an excellent column on this subject last Thursday. If you missed it you should go back and read it. She was a Red and Black staff member and holds a degree from the University Journalism School, you know, and is far more capable than I to write about what goes on up there.

During his time at Georgia, son David joined the ROTC and spent the summer before his senior year training at Quantico, Virginia. The day of his graduation from the University, he was commissioned a Marine Corps second lieutenant and became the husband of Beverly Fegal, his college sweetheart. In time they would become the parents of a son, Mark Robert, and a daughter Julie Anne.

Meanwhile, younger brother Ralph had taken up where David left off on Carrollton's football team. Tall and slender like his father, and *his* father before him, Ralph became a star running back for the Trojans. He also excelled at track and won the State Championship in the 220 his senior year. He became the first athlete from Carrollton to add pole vaulting to his running, but early in the season he took a hard fall, injuring his left arm. The treatment for this injury all but stopped the muscle development in his upper arm.

"That injury affected his football playing some," Stanley said. "But Florida State gave him a scholarship when he graduated from high school."

Ralph moved to Tallahassee for his freshman year of college. But due to over-recruiting by the coaches and his increasing inability to use his left arm, he lost the scholarship. He returned to Carrollton and enrolled at West Georgia College, later graduating.

While serving three years active duty in the Marines, David was scheduled to participate in support of the Bay of Pigs mission, an attempt by the United States to overthrow the Castro regime. "They were on their way to Florida when it was called off," remembered Stanley. "I was really worried for him; it was what you call a close one."

Out of the marines, David and Beverly returned to Carrollton where David became editor of the *Bremen Gateway,* and later, during the problems in Douglasville, transferred to the *Sentinel.* But life had another plan for David. He was soon offered a position in Public Relations at West Georgia College, where he would remain until his retirement.

With David's assistance, Ralph secured a similar position with Stetson University. After a time, he left Stetson and returned to Carrollton where Stanley had a new endeavor awaiting him.

Several citizens from the Oxford, Alabama, area had expressed interest in a newspaper of their own besides the *Anniston Star.* As a result Stanley met with potential stockholders and ultimately agreed to start the *Oxford Sun.* Ralph, now married to Beth Johnson and the father of a son, Mel, became the editor.

In the meantime, Jack Wood, one of the Oxford stockholders and owner of the nearby Helflin, Alabama, *Cleburne News,* convinced Stanley to buy his paper. "We were already printing it for him," Stanley recalled, "so we added it to our organization."

CHAPTER XX

THE SISTERS PARKMAN

For some reason, I can't recall as much about the girls when they were growing up, probably because they were more into piano lessons and that sort of thing, whereas the boys played sports, and I always covered their games for the paper. But I've got two great daughters, I'll tell you that.

Patricia, or Patti, as she was called, was well aware of her father's fondness of sports. So she joined her high school basketball team, despite having no real interest in playing. She was tall like her father and brothers, but her height could not compensate for her indifference to the game.

Patti's coach put her in during a game that Stanley had come to watch, and she fouled out before the end of the first half. Stanley recalled, "She was afraid I was going to criticize her for being such a poor player, but instead I bragged on her for being so aggressive!"

Patti graduated from Carrollton High School in 1960. By that time, West Georgia College had become a four-year institution, and Patti enrolled to pursue a teaching degree. Stanley recalled, "It was no big secret that Patti and her mother didn't get along real well during those teenage years. And by the time she graduated from high school, I guess she had stayed home about as long as she could stand."

With some girlfriends, Patti moved into a rental house in nearby Roopville. But after her freshman year of college, she realized the inconvenience of driving back and forth every day and returned to her parents' home, which was located across the street from the campus. Patti received her teaching degree in 1964, and began her classroom career in Gainesville. After a while, she moved to Smyrna, then to North Roswell. She married Bill Laufler, an adjustor with C&A Insurance, and the couple moved to various cities as the company transferred him.

Laufler's parents had immigrated to the U. S. from Germany years before. He was well over six feet tall and had played basketball for Seton Hall the year they won the National Championship.

For a time, Patti and Bill lived in Los Angeles, California, where Patti had a humorous encounter. She applied for a teaching position, and during an interview, the administrator complemented Patti on her resume, but ended the conversation by saying, "The only problem I see is that you need to learn to speak English."

Stanley laughed, "They didn't appreciate her southern drawl, but she later won the Teacher of the Year Award in that school system. I'd say she learned English!"

Patti's marriage to Bill ended in divorce. She moved to Pinellas County, Florida, and continued teaching. There she married King McLaurin, a graduate of the Citadel, who was also an insurance adjustor. But, sadly, after a few years, McLaurin developed lung cancer and later died. Time passed and Patti married Ted Burlage, also in the insurance business. Their marriage was a lasting one.

Unlike Patti, younger sister Carroll never tried her luck at high school basketball. Instead, she excelled in music, playing piano and the alto saxophone in the marching band. When she was fifteen, she entered the Miss Carrollton Beauty Pageant and walked away with the crown.

"Much to my regret," Stanley said, "no member of the family was there when she won. Frances was sick in bed, and I had stayed home with her."

Carroll graduated from Carrollton High School in 1964, and, like her siblings before her, enrolled at West Georgia College. In a freshman English course she made an "F" on her first writing assignment. To compound matters, the professor attached a note: "I can't believe that a Parkman did so poorly in writing this paper."

Carroll was livid. Stanley recalled, "She came home that afternoon and slammed that paper down and said, 'I'm leaving that college as soon as I can.'"

In the end, however, Carroll passed the course with a "B." But there was more about West Georgia that managed to rile her. "Patti was a popular senior when Carroll was a freshman," said Stanley, "and Carroll got tired of walking into the student center and everyone saying, 'Look, there's Patti's little sister.'"

While at West Georgia, Carroll began dating Claude Wills. Together they transferred to the University of Georgia and married. Carroll took a position with C&S Bank in Atlanta, and Claude worked for CNS Insurance Organization. They became the parents of a son, Preston Parkman. After a few years, Claude's job required them to transfer to Birmingham, Alabama. There, Carroll began an eighteen-year career with Coldwell Banker, which culminated in her retirement.

CHAPTER XXI

MANAGING THE NEWSPAPER

I was lucky to have a great group of people working for me in those days. Hiram Bray was my News Editor, and others like Mary Eason were tireless in making sure everything ran smoothly. We often asked ourselves how we made it through all we had to deal with.

In 1962, Hiram Bray was doing radio news for Carrollton's WLBB radio station when the owners sold out to a new group. "The new owner took over at 5 o'clock, and I was gone at 5:01," Bray recalled.

Bray was a young man with a family to support. He, too, was a graduate of the University of Georgia Journalism School and knew as much about newspaper work as he did about radio.

"He called about me giving him a job," said Stanley, "and I told him to meet me at my office on Sunday afternoon and we'd talk." Bray recalled, "He asked me only one question: 'Can you type?' I told him I learned to type in the Navy in WWII, so he told me to be there Monday morning, and I never missed a lick of work. That was the beginning of the best fifty years of my life."

Bray, it turned out, was a capable and skilled reporter. He covered such controversial topics as the integration of the Carroll County Schools, and the arrest of a prominent doctor for allegedly altering official police records. He also became famous for his humorous writing about mythological "Ploughshare, Georgia." Over the next decades, Bray added an extra dimension to the *Georgian*.

Bray remembered, "In all the years I worked for Stanley he got on me only once, and that was indirectly. When he hired me, he didn't know that I was a Republican. There were only about five or six in the whole town. So if one walked down the street, I'd put it on the front page of the paper. One day I turned to the editorial page as always to see what he had to say. The first line slapped me right across the face: 'Dear Newspaper Readers, let me make one thing clear; this is not a Republican newspaper!' He never said a word to me, but I sure got the hint!" Hiram Bray passed away in June 2005 as this book was being written.

During the years, tough situations arose that Stanley had to deal with. One of the earliest occurred in the late forties and involved the murder of a prominent young man near the Sunset Hills area. The murder provoked widespread fear and anger among Carrollton residents, and acting as a responsible news organ the Georgian covered the story in detail and promoted community involvement in helping to solve the crime.

Citizens did not criticize this line of reporting. However, Carrollton's Chief of Police, Rada Threadgill, became angry at what he saw as "hasty reporting" and confronted Stanley.

Stanley recalled, "He had previously requested that I not carry rape cases in the paper, to which I agreed. But when that murder occurred, I carried it in the next issue. Apparently, Threadgill had assumed I would still abide by his orders and not report this crime."

Chief Threadgill was fuming when he came into Stanley's office. He yanked his pistol from its holster and his badge from his uniform, lay both on the desk, and ordered Stanley to follow him out to the parking where he intended to "beat hell" out of him.

"I said, 'Well Rada, there is a murderer loose in this town, and I have no apologies to make about the story. Now you can beat me up, but I'm not going outside of this building whether you've got your gun on or not. And as soon as I have the strength to get to the telephone, I'm going to call the sheriff to put you in jail, and I'll have another story to put in the paper."

Needless to say, Stanley left the office that day without a scratch, and Threadgill stopped trying to exercise power over the newspaper.

The following is excerpted from a front page story in the *Carroll County Georgian,* Thursday, November 4, 1948:

ONE SUSPECT HELD, NO NEW CLUES AS STEVENS' MURDERER IS SOUGHT

Angered uncertainty is still the feeling of Carrollton people today as the search continues for clues that will answer the question of what brutal murderer killed Carl Stevens, Jr. Sunday night near the Sunset Hills residential section of the city as he sought to defend his young lady companion.

Stevens, 22, a student at Georgia Tech, was the only son of Mr. and Mrs. Carl Stevens Sr. of Carrollton. His companion, whom he sought to defend, is a student at LaGrange College and the two were visiting their parents in Carrollton for the weekend.

Here is the story of what happened, as it has been related by the hysterical young woman who as a popular member of the younger set was crowned beauty queen of Carrollton three years ago.

The young couple had parked his Plymouth sedan at the end of Sunset Blvd., a half block to the rear of the home of Judge Samuel J. Boykin and a block from the location of the Stevens' new home in Sunset Hills residential section.

According to the story recounted by the young lady, they were listening to the automobile radio when the assailant walked up to the car pointed a gun in the window at them and commanded her to remove her shoes, and both of them get out of the car.

The radio was left playing and was still on when officers located the car about two hours later. The assailant kept the gun pointed at the couple and marched them across a nearby cotton field to a thick growth of trees about a half mile away. Stevens carried the girl most of the distance to prevent severe injury to her to her bare feet walking across the rocky ground.

As the assailant attempted to attack the young girl, Stevens lunged for him and the two engaged in a bitter struggle as the valiant young man told the girl to run. When she was some distance away she said she heard the three shots.

Making her way to the residential section of Griffin Avenue, about 400 yards from the scene of the crime, she reported what had happened to George Syme, whose home she reached first.

Mr. Syme called Sheriff B.B. Kilgore at about 10 o'clock, according to the sheriff. Mr. Kilgore rushed to the Syme home, rounded up a few assistants, and tried to follow the directions given by the girl, in locating young Stevens. The directions were difficult to follow in the total darkness as the distressed girl bravely tried to direct the searching party. Finally it was necessary to find her tracks and trace them back over the route she had taken in her flight. Finally when the body of the victim was located it was about an hour and a half after the sheriff had been called.

The popular Carrollton boy had been shot three times. The bullet which apparently caused his instant death had been fired at extremely close range and traveled through his chest. Other bullet wounds were in his arm and leg.

As rapidly as possible posses were formed of angered Carrollton citizens and searches were launched in the vicinity of the attack. Bloodhounds were brought from Fulton and Cobb counties but due to a rain that had been falling during the evening, the

dogs were unable to strike a trail.

By early morning hours the city was shocked with the news and organized searching parties, under the direction of Georgia Highway Patrolmen and the Georgia Bureau of Investigation, were combing the entire area.

Other situations proved less dire. During the Vietnam War, the *Georgian* printed a birth announcement presented by a young mother in which she named the father of her new pride and joy. Shortly after, this young man walked into the newspaper office and demanded that the announcement be retracted.

Stanley recalled the awkward moment: "The boy said, 'That ain't my baby. I was in Vietnam when that baby was conceived!' I told him, 'Well, it's going to be pretty hard for me to retract the birth of a baby!'"

CHAPTER XXII

FOR EVERYTHING A SEASON

The saddest day of my life was when Frances died. It happened suddenly, without warning, and I was simply in shock. We buried her on Christmas Eve, which only increased our sorrow. It was a hard, difficult time.

For most of her life Frances Parkman suffered migraine headaches. Some were so severe that she had to have injections to sleep, at times for days. She had made peace with this adversity, however, and managed to live a full and eventful life.

In late December, 1971, Frances and Mary Eason were performing their usual morning proofreading in their separate office at the newspaper when something happened.

Stanley recalled the moment well: "About mid-morning Mary Eason came to my office and said, 'Mrs. Parkman is having some kind of attack, and you need to come see about her.' So I ran down there, and she was still conscious, but she was awfully foggy."

Stanley helped Frances to walk to the car and drove her to the emergency room. Dr. Sonny Bass examined her and concluded her condition was migraine-related. He advised that she lie down in the E. R. until she felt well enough to go home.

But by the time Dr. Bass made it to the end of the hall, Frances was unconscious. An aneurism was immediately diagnosed, and an emergency tracheotomy was performed to restore her breathing. Frances remained comatose.

Later that night, Dr. Bass recommended that Frances be seen by a brain specialist at Emory Hospital in Atlanta. The specialist was called, but he explained to Stanley that he did not drive after dark, and it was past midnight. He'd be there first thing the next morning. Two of Stanley's friends, Charles Willis and Roger Miles, knew that time was of the essence. They sped to the doctor's home and brought him back to Carrollton where he joined the other doctors who examined Frances. After long consultation, the physicians concluded that nothing could be done to save her.

Stanley recalled the moment, saying, "Patti was the only one of the children not present. She flew in the following day, and the family made the difficult decision to give them permission to remove Frances from life support. She was only fifty-six."

Frances' funeral was held on Christmas Eve, 1971, and was attended by many newspaper people, friends, and others, including, Sam Griffin, President of the Georgia Press Association, and his wife. She was laid to rest at Carroll Memory Gardens.

CHAPTER XXIII

A CIVIC DUTY

> When we came to Carrollton I didn't join any civic clubs immediately. But as time went on, I became involved in many of the major service projects and charitable works in the area. I suppose you could call it a civic duty.

In addition to his involvement in the Chamber of Commerce, the Rotary Club, and the Recreation Department, Stanley also accepted other civic roles over the years.

One of those roles was in connection to an election and, ironically, to Stanley's failure to follow his own good advice never to endorse a political candidate.

Horry Duncan was running for County Commissioner, and Stanley, through the *Georgian,* endorsed another candidate who had already served a four-year term in that office. When Duncan was elected, Stanley responded with an editorial congratulating him on his victory and wishing him best of luck during his term. "I also added that I would give him a year or two to prove himself and would have more to say after he had done so," said a smiling Stanley.

From that time on when Duncan encountered Stanley, his first words were, "Well, Stanley, have I proved myself yet?"

What happened next to Stanley in this matter involved the Hospital Authority, which, from its start, had been chaired by Roy Richards. Now elected commissioner, Duncan convinced the Georgia Legislature to pass a bill limiting the time that any person could serve as chairman to three, three year terms, for a total of nine. Since Richards had already served ten years as chairman, his term was immediately up. This fact established, Duncan approached Stanley about filling the now unoccupied position.

"Horry asked if I would serve on the Hospital Authority and I told him I'd be happy to," Stanley recounted. "Then he told me I'd be replacing Roy Richards, and I quickly told him that I'd serve as Chairman but not, under any circumstances, for the term following Roy, for obvious reasons."

So Duncan enlisted Hugh Brock, a local farmer, to succeed Richards for the remainder of the term. When it was up in 1973, he appointed Stanley Chairman.

And the tale continues...

During his Chairmanship, Stanley and Duncan eventually became friends. "But he was a stubborn, hard-boiled, difficult politician," Stanley groused, "and if I asked him for a favor, he'd often tell me no without blinking an eye."

Once a year, though, Stanley had to go, hat in hand, to County Commissioner Duncan and plead for funds, because the county, which had the funds, did not subsidize the hospital. The amount of $50,000 was desperately needed.

Despite the fact that he was a stubborn, hard-boiled, difficult politician, and it was not in his county budget, Duncan always gave the Authority the money requested,

In addition to his service on the Hospital Authority, Stanley was on the board of directors of the Chattahoochee Flint Area Planning and Development Association, which played a vital role in the long-range economic planning for the counties of Troop, Heard, Carroll, Coweta and Haralson.

CHAPTER XXIV

TIMES THEY ARE CHANGING

After a few years we sold the *Oxford Sun* to a group who wanted to turn it into a regional shopper, and Ralph then came to Carrollton as our Advertising Director. Other changes were under way, also, in my personal life.

Mary Pass had been a widow for five years when she met Stanley Parkman. Her husband, Floyd, had died of cancer, leaving her to raise their two teenage children alone.

By the early seventies their son Jerry was attending West Georgia College, and their daughter, Milah, was in high school at Carrollton. Mary worked as an X-ray technician with Tanner Medical Center, and was also employed by Carroll EMC.

Her son, Jerry Richard Pass, was born June 28, 1947, in Griffin, Georgia, where the family had made their home. When he was eighteen-months-old, the Passes relocated to Carrollton, where Floyd started his own plumbing business. Daughter, Milah Faith, was born in Carrollton on May 21, 1953. Both children attended Carrollton schools, with Jerry excelling in football and playing the alto saxophone in the band. The years following Floyd's death proved a difficult time for Mary. Jerry joined the army after graduating from college and was sent to

Vietnam. Mary felt the emotional strain of the absence of her husband, her daughter still in high school, and her son, the only male member of the family, in mortal danger half-way around the world.

It had been two years since Frances Parkman had passed away, and Stanley had not even thought about the prospect of dating. But Hiram Bray, his friend and News Editor for the *Georgian*, had thought about it for him.

Stanley recounted, "Hiram, in his low-key way of doing things, came in my office one day and said, 'Stanley, why don't you get a date with Mary Pass? She's single, she's attractive, she's president of the Pilot Club. I think you ought to get to know her.'"

At the time, Stanley was still involved in the Manchester newspaper and was driving there at least once a week to tend to business. During one trip there he spent the night at a hotel in Warm Springs and from his room mustered up the courage to call Mary.

"I was scared to death," he recalled. "After saying hello and chatting a minute, I said, 'How about having dinner with me Friday night?' But she said, 'I can't Friday because my son Jerry is getting married, and I've got a shower to attend in Metter.' So I said I'd call her later."

A few weeks later he did, and the two drove to Atlanta for dinner. When they got back to Carrollton, they made another date.

Mary recalled, "After a few dates where he walked me to my front door to say goodbye, he asked, 'Do you ever invite anybody inside your house for coffee?' so I figured it was time to have him over to meet Milah and have dinner."

"Sometime after that," Stanley remembered, "I asked Hiram if he thought it'd be all right for me to ask Mary to marry me. He made a big smile said, 'Yes! That's the thing to do!'"

Stanley had to work up his courage. When he did, he wasted no time and picked up the phone and popped the question. Mary, however, insisted on a face-to-face proposal.

So Stanley got up his courage again, went to her house, and Mary agreed to become his wife.

On April 6, 1973, the two were married in a service at the Christian Church where Mary attended. David, Ralph and Jerry stood up for their parents. After a small reception, the newlyweds honeymooned in San Francisco. Stanley recalled, "The hotel was way up on a hill where the cable cars are. We rode around on them, and we ate at the Fisherman's Wharf a few times."

Not long after returning to Carrollton, they made plans to build a house all their own. Mary sold her house, and she and Stanley moved into the apartment that David and Beverly were renting. David and Beverly moved into Stanley's house. Eventually, Stanley and Mary found a tract of land they liked just out of town and large enough for Stanley to cultivate a garden. Within a year they moved into their spacious custom-designed home.

Mary continued to work in order to repay a loan from People's Bank that she had taken for Jerry and Milah's college tuition. Stanley recalled, "She positively would not hear of me repaying that loan for her. And that spoke volumes to me about her character."

Jerry came home from Vietnam and completed his service as a 1st Lieutenant. He took a job with Equitable Life Insurance Company in Atlanta where he eventually became Agency Manager. He had married Lynn Moore of Metter, Georgia, shortly before Mary and Stanley's first date. They would become the parents of a son, Richard Wesley. Later they moved to Columbia, South Carolina, where Jerry ran his own Equitable agency, from which he eventually retired. He and Lynn settled in Marietta, Georgia.

Milah graduated from Carrollton High School in 1971 and attended West Georgia College for a year and a half before transferring to Piedmont Nursing School. After six months there, she was accepted into the Medical College of Georgia where she would receive a Bachelor's degree in nursing. She worked as a charge nurse at Tanner Memorial Hospital, and later married Steve Lynn from LaGrange, Georgia.

Upon marrying Lynn, Milah relocated with him to Louis-ville, Kentucky, then to California, Oklahoma and, finally, Nash-ville, Tennessee. She worked as a nurse in the various cities in which they lived, and while in Oklahoma City started her own business, called Nanny & New Born, which was wildly successful.

The Lynns' became the parents of a daughter, Laura Whit-ney, and a son, Joshua Jarred.

1973 found Stanley happier than he'd been in more than two years. With his new extended family, he resolved to make them just as happy.

CHAPTER XXV

END OF AN ERA

> When my dad died, I was recovering from a heart attack and couldn't go to his funeral. He and I had never been able to communicate as much as I would have liked, but I admired and respected him. He was without doubt the best man I've ever known.

In the fall of 1978, Stanley experienced some heart palpitations, and his doctor referred him to Emory Hospital's Cardiology Group, headed by Dr. Willis Hearst, a native of Carrollton. Dr. Steve Clements of the Group performed an arteriogram on him, which necessitated an overnight stay for recovery. Late that evening, he suffered a heart attack.

He recalled the moment, saying, "They rushed me down to intensive care, and the next morning when I regained consciousness, there were about four or five doctors in white coats standing around my bed. Well, I thought I'd died and gone to heaven, and they were a host of angels!"

In actuality the medical host were discussing Stanley's condition. They decided the best treatment was a course of medication rather than surgery. After several more days in the hospital, he went home to convalesce, and it was then that his father, Stanley Parkman, Sr., passed away at age ninety-two and was buried in Columbus, Georgia.

Stanley recalled, "Mary and I had visited him down in Chattahoochee the weekend before my heart attack. He wasn't doing well then, so his death was not that unexpected."

Parkman had made a special request to Stanley a month before he passed away:

"He said to me, 'Stanley, I know I'm not going to live a whole lot longer, and I've never been able to do what I'm going to ask you. After remarrying, it just was not appropriate for me to talk about your mother. Consequently, her grave never had any attention. As soon as you have the opportunity, please find her grave and have it cleaned up real nice. I'd like to know you're going to do that.'"

Stanley promised that he would. Mary took the initiative in finding Alice's gravesite and, together, they had a border built around its perimeter, added a headstone, and placed flowers.

Two years after the death of his father, Stanley's step-mother, Frances, succumbed to Alzheimer's disease and was buried beside her husband in Columbus.

But this period was not to end on a sad note. In the spring of 1980, Stanley made a decision that would become the climax of his years of hard work.

CHAPTER XXVI

TO REAP WHAT YOU SOW

> I could never get Roy Richards or Lynn Holmes to
> sell me their interests in the paper. So I came to the
> conclusion that the only way in the world I was
> going to get my share of what the organization
> was worth was to sell it to somebody else.

The CEO of Hart Hank Communications Company was a
Georgian and a graduate of the University of Georgia School
of Journalism. The company headquarters was in Corpus
Christie, Texas, but since the CEO was partial to Georgia, the
company had purchased the Monroe paper when its owners
retired.

"I wrote the CEO a letter in a rather jovial mood one day,"
Stanley recalled. "It said, 'You've bought one Georgia paper;
how about buying the best?'"

Within a week, Stanley was contacted by John Ginn, the
Vice President of Hart Hanks out of Anderson, South Carolina.
They had a meeting, and Ginn wasted little time making an
offer that made Stanley catch his breath. "I was shocked,"
Stanley admitted. "The figure was much more than I had ever
dreamed it would be."

Soon after that, Larry Franklin, the Hart Hanks Chief Financial Officer, arrived in Carrollton with four checks in his briefcase: one was made out to Roy Richards, one to Lynn Holmes, one to Mrs. Jewel, widow of Dr. Roberts, and one to Stanley Parkman.

With the understanding that Stanley would remain as Publisher for at least two years, the deal appeared to be done. But Roy Richards was having second thoughts.

"He walked up and down the hall of that law office for an hour at least, thinking we were making a big mistake in selling,"Stanley said.

After a while, Larry Franklin grew impatient and issued an ultimatum. He would remain for ten minutes, and if the deal wasn't completed, he was going home and taking the checks with him.

Stanley was frantic.

But Richards was the first to speak: "Stanley, I think we're making a mistake. But if you really want to sell, I'll sign the papers, but only after you do."

Stanley said: "Hand me the pen!"

Continuing as Publisher, Stanley now had another problem to deal with. The new owners wanted to change the *Georgian* to a daily, but no member of the staff, including Stanley, had experience running one. The solution was that Hart Hanks sent Bill Martin from the Monroe paper to be General Manager. By November the paper was being printed daily as *The Times Georgian*.

Stanley was Publisher and Bill Martin was General Manager for seven more years, five years longer than Stanley expected. Then, in 1987, Hart Hanks sold the Carrollton organization. Stanley reflected, "By that time, I had no business as Publisher anyway, but the new owners allowed me to keep my office there in the building, which I appreciated."

Hart Hanks had another assignment for Bill Martin in Texas. On his way out of the office for the last time, he placed a hand-written note on Stanley's desk: "I am proud to have had the relationship that I have had with you for these past seven years. You mean more to me than any other man alive outside of my father."

"Reading Bill's words," Stanley recalled, speaking slowly, "was one of the proud moments of my life."

It was during this winning period of Stanley's life that son Ralph was elected to the Georgia State Legislature. His first marriage had ended in divorce, and he married to Joanne Lovvorn of Carrollton. After serving two terms, Ralph and Joanne moved to

Florida where they started their own business.

CHAPTER XXVII

CONTINUED FAITH

I owe everything in my professional and personal life to my faith in God and the church. I always strive to be a good Christian, knowing there is always room for improvement, and trying to remain humble in the face of all my blessings.

Since his introduction to the Baptist faith as a child in Hardaway, Florida, Stanley remained steadfast in his quest to be a worthy Christian. In Carrollton, he committed himself to a local church, the First Baptist, just as he had in the prior communities in which he lived. He would be a deacon at First Baptist for more than fifty years and serve for several years as Superintendent of Sunday School. He also taught a Sunday school class for men, for a time alongside future Speaker of the House Newt Gingrich.

In 1995 Stanley was asked to lead the pulpit committee that brought Reverend Steve Davis to Carrollton. Stanley recalled, "As I was reading over Steve's resume, I noticed that he had as a reference Eric Holliman, who was the pastor of the First Baptist Church in Quincy, Florida."

Surprised to see the name of his old town, Stanley called Holliman. He explained to the young man that he had been a deacon in the Quincy church more than fifty years prior, and the two recalled church members they both knew. Holliman recommended Steve Davis "without reservations", and Stanley invited Davis to Carrollton. "He was the first person I spoke with from Carrollton," said Davis. "He had the respect of his church, and I was very impressed by that."

As chairman of the search committee and elder statesman of the church, it was under Stanley's initiative that Davis was chosen to be the pastor of Carrollton First Baptist.

Davis soon became even more impressed by Stanley's poised leadership. "Stanley was and is the person people look to when there is a big decision to be made" he said. "In meetings he is generally quiet, taking everything in, and after a while he will stand to his feet to speak, and everybody listens."

Around the same time that Davis accepted the call to First Baptist, the congregation began "Vision 2000," a campaign for renovating the church buildings.

Under the joint leadership of Stanley and Mary, the campaign goals were met. In a display of gratitude, the church secretly decided to name a room in their honor.

Stanley recalled the ceremony in which the room was dedicated: "All of the kids had come to church with us, and I thought how odd it was that we were all together for once. But they knew what was going on. At the end of the church service, I was stunned to hear *The Parkman Room* announced."

"He is a beloved member of this church," said Davis, "and my wife and I love him so very much. He is a great, great man and a faithful Christian."

CHAPTER XXVIII

THE LATER YEARS

Mary and I both served on the board of the American Heart Association for thirty-five years. She took on the responsibility of spear-heading the Jump Rope for Heart fundraisers in the local schools, and we were twice honored as Heart Association Couple of the Year.

As time passed, Stanley relinquished many of his civic roles, focusing his attention on his weekly editorials for the *Times Georgian* and cultivating a good-sized plot behind his house. "I've always liked to see things grow," he said, "and I really enjoy my garden."

He bought equipment and supplies from Burson's Feed and Seed and planted a variety of vegetables, including tomatoes, pole beans, yellow and zucchini squashes, and okra. He even had a well bored especially for the garden. Mary canned much of the produce and became famous within the family for her tomatoes, which she used to make chili and other dishes.

In 1990 the Sertoma Club presented Stanley with its "Service to Mankind Award," which he received with great appreciation.

Stanley's brother Tol passed away quietly in his sleep in the early nineties at his home in Chattahoochee where he had made his living as a farmer. His two sisters, however, were living successful lives of their own. The oldest, Frances, had graduated from the University of Tennessee and become a popular math teacher. She lived with her husband and children in Nashville, Tennessee. Jane, the youngest, also was a college graduate, receiving her music degree from Florida State University and going on to enjoy a thriving career as a music teacher. Her home was in Cuthbert, Georgia.

In 2005, members of the community organized a banquet at which Stanley was honored for his many years of service to society. Held in a large room at the college, it was attended by more than 200 people, including close family and friends.

Stanley attributed his health and longevity to God's grace and his father's good genes, and looked back on his life with satisfaction. "I don't know of anybody I'd want to change places with," he said. "I don't envy anybody; I *sure* don't envy the Prince of Wales! I don't have much time left in my life, but even if I did, I wouldn't start a new career. I'm happy the way it is"

He paused; after a moment's thought, he smiled and said, "I have what I need to live, and for me, that's plenty."

CHAPTER XXIX

EDITORIALLY SPEAKING

WONDER AT THE MYSTERIES OF THE GARDEN
by Stanley Parkman
(The *Times Georgian*, Sunday, June 30, 2002)

The home gardening season in Carroll County is well under way for this year and some of it (for the better gardeners) is moving into the harvesting period but I am still getting such questions as: Do you have a garden this year? Did you reduce your garden size like you vowed to do? What do you have planted this year? What are you doing about the crows, rabbits, coons and deer? How are you handling the weather conditions?

All of these questions come with facial expressions and voice tones that are really saying, "You should have learned by now that you are no gardener and you should be smart enough to stop trying!"

Add to that the fact that I have learned that we can buy vegetables that we need for about one-third of what is spent on my gardening—not considering the labor and aggravation.

But, on the other hand I still need the exercise and am still trying to understand the mysteries encountered in my gardening efforts. As stated before, every succeeding year brings greater appreciation for the farmers and their faith, fortitude and courage in pursuing such a risky way of earning a livelihood.

There are such mysteries as these—all encountered already this season: 1. How can you know when to plant with weather and soil conditions varying every spring? 2. Why will the squash grow poorly for several years and this year, under less favorable conditions, produce more that the past three years combined? 3. Why will a 100-foot row of peas planted the same day, under exactly the same conditions, have half the row come up and not a single plant on the other half of the row? Now, replanted 45 days later, the other half has come up well. 4. Why did the beans germinate well in soil that was clean and prepared just right but now the weeds can't be pulled out without also pulling up the bean plants?

All of us "good old gardeners" know that most of the planting in our area should be done on Good Friday. Well, this year we had heavy rains during the two weeks before Good Friday and I had to wait an extra two weeks for the soil to dry out enough to plant. In the meantime Carl Brack and Horace Johnson (two of my gardening experts and friends) had corn up 8 to 10 inches tall. Maybe it is because they are about four miles further south and they have that special magic.

After Good Friday and my soil was dry enough, we had about three weeks of dry, hot weather and nothing will germinate under those conditions. But then the rains came and we praised the Lord for it but we didn't need five inches of it in two days. As a result most of the stuff that had not germinated in the dry soil was then covered with top-soil and mud. The corn didn't need the plastic netting we had spread over it for protection from the crows because it was then too deep for the crows to dig up or to germinate.

So, in answer to frequent questions: Yes, I prepared and planted as much as ever, some of it was planted for the third time and still has not come up. Okra, cucumbers and peas were planted three times and finally had to be thinned and their productivity is still very much in question. Half the watermelons came up but none of the cantaloupes. Potatoes may produce half a crop but beets did not make it at all. Butterbeans are completely overwhelmed by grass and weeds—two hoes and a tiller are broken and the repair shop can't get to it because of overwork.

Two drilled wells provide ample water for irrigation but there is too much expense and labor to get it on a large garden and the water is just right for grass and weeds. Besides the visiting cranes have made a great landing field of the fish pond where they really appreciate the supply of young, restocked catfish.

The one thing that I have had in overabundance is BIRTH-DAYS and I'm thankful for every one of them.

A FATHER DETERMINES "THE GOOD OLD DAYS"
by Stanley Parkman
(The *Times Georgian,* Sunday, November 3, 2002)

Today is June 16, designated on our calendars as "Father's Day" and you readers would normally expect something related to the observance of this special day. Unfortunately, I don't have any words of wisdom that have not been used before and often.

So often you have heard and read the thoughts of those in my generation as we told of the "good old days" being so much better than life and habits of today and the two generations that have followed. But then as I dig deep into my heart and try to compare myself to my Dad and to my sons and grandsons, I find very little, if anything, that puts me ahead in any comparison.

The conclusion is that I don't grade out as well as my Dad and his generation and my grade is lower than those of my sons and grandsons. So what does that leave for me to write about on this Father's Day?

My Dad was born to poor parents in South Georgia and grew up in rural areas under very modest economic conditions, and so did I and so did my sons. My mother died when I was

5 years of age and my Dad's mother died when he was young. My Dad's formal education reached only through about the sixth grade and mine extended through high school but he was better educated that I through his own studying and reading. My sons and grandsons have college educations or will have, so the younger generations have that advantage.

The material rewards of life—food, clothing, homes, vehicles have been better for my generation than for my Dad's but so are they better for sons and grandsons.

Healthcare, medicines, and physical comforts of life have improved as years have passed, but Dad lived to be 92 and had less illness than I have had and all of us "youngsters" just pray that we will match his age and physical well being.

Faith in God, or deep religious belief, is probably the greatest possession that any individual of any generation can claim and none of us can come up to Dad's mark on that.

So, where does that leave me in trying to provoke thoughts about "the good old days" in relation to Father's Day, 2002?

I'll tell you about "the good old days"—they are determined by the individual who is living at the time, regardless of the generation or the year on the calendar. The good days for any father are the days in which he lives and are judged by the kind of man he is in the eyes of his family, his friends, his community and his God.

If it is determined that "the good old days" of my family history were during the lifetime of my Dad, then it was because he made them so with the resources, talents and gifts that God gave him rather than the economic conditions or the customs of his day.

There is a good probability that the years of my sons and grandsons will be better classified as "the good old days" than those of my Dad but it will be made so by each of them, individually, rather than by the environment in which they live.

The thought for this Father's Day is that every father in America could and should be living in "the good old days" of his family history because he is making the best of the resources, talents and gifts that God has given him.

Have a great day, all of you!

ET'-STYLE REPORTING WATERS DOWN NEWS
by Stanley Parkman
(The *Times Georgian,* Sunday, May 18, 2003)

It was a pleasant surprise when the Whitesburg Elementary School string ensemble was introduced as the program for the Carrollton Rotary Club at noon Tuesday.

The program had not been previously announced and most of the Rotarians had no idea such a talented young group had been organized.

These are students who are in the fifth or lower grades, and several of those performing have only been in the program one year. Part of the financing for their instruments came from a small grant that was arranged by Rep. Tracy Stallings while he was in the Georgia General Assembly.

The group is taught and directed by Beverly Noell who has been on the Whitesburg Elementary faculty about four years. In proudly introducing members of the ensemble, she mentioned the fifth-graders will be moving on to Central Middle School next year but intend to continue their participation in the school music program.

Friday is the last day of school for this term, which has seemed to be extremely short for adults but long and tiring for students. Many of the students who are anxious for summer vacation are also proud to demonstrate advances they have made in public education this term. These young people give enthusiasm, life and hope for our future while we adults get bogged down in politics, greed and negative attitudes that lead us to cynicism and wars with little positive good accomplished.

This probably will sound like a confusing column to many of you and the truth of the matter is that it is confusing to me—the writer.

In this age of information and communication, it has become more difficult to sort out what is the truth and what is fiction, advertising, public relations or politics. And since it is more and more difficult to determine the truth, it is helpful and refreshing to see and hear something like a performance of the Whitesburg Elementary School string ensemble or a home run in the ninth inning of a Braves baseball game. When I immediately see and hear something like that or a great anthem by the church choir, I know that I am seeing and hearing the truth and not propaganda.

I am thankful for newspapers and performances on the stages or the playing fields of amateur organizations.

There have been dire predictions that new communications technology will drive newspapers from the media scene, but during the most recent 75 years that has not happened. The reason it has not happened is that most all other media has become more "entertainment" than "news and information."

The TV talk shows, for example, have become forums for illogical debate and entertainment rather than news, and they compete over the same stories to the neglect of everything else that is happening around the world. And, getting at the truth of a matter is absolutely impossible.

Contrary to this, you can read the facts in the newspaper and make your own decisions. If you don't get it in the first reading, you can read it again at your leisure.

I still have some questions about the war in Iraq. I don't know whether it was for the ridding of Saddam Hussein and weapons of mass destruction—neither of which have been found—or was it for the benefit of re-electing President George W. Bush?

I am also getting weary of President Bush and others in his administration making all these glowing promises of letting some dominate the formation of their new government and taking the profits from the rebuilding of the country.

I am solidly opposed to the price America has paid for the liberation of the people of Iraq, and then turn it over to the same kind of tyrants our military forces have already defeated.

The people of Iraq and their neighbors can keep their cultures of food, religion, dress and other such matters if they want, but I am in favor of "an eye for an eye and a tooth for a tooth" or two eyes and two teeth for every one when it comes to killing Americans or British now that the Iraqis have been liberated.

I put more confidence in a performance of the Whitesburg Elementary string ensemble at the Rotary Club than I do in Larry King's panel of experts telling me who killed Laci Peterson and her baby in California.

ABOUT THE AUTHOR

Stanley Parkman is the Pulisher - Editor Emerritus of the Times-Georgian newspaper in Carrollton, Georgia. Regarded by many to be one of the finest stewards of community newspapers in Georgia, Stanley and his wfe Mary live in Carrollton, Georgia. Stanley Parkman continues to maintain and active office and role in the newspaper he founded when not tending to his garden at home.

Printed in the United States
59512LVS00005B/79-96